IN
MEMORIAM

IN
MEMORIAM

Edited by Michael Wynn Jones

Some
obituaries
on the passing
of some cherished
ideas, institutions
and ways
of life

Hodder & Stoughton

LLOYD'S
LLOYD'S OF LONDON

Thanks, for their help in the production of this book,
to Brian Nicholson, Peter Hill, Mark Whitfield,
Victoria Cripps, Sarah Goddard, and Delina Rees

British Library Cataloguing-in-Publication Data

In memoriam.
  I. Wynn Jones, Michael
  828

  ISBN   0-340-56201-3

First published in Great Britain 1991
Copyright © Lloyd's of London 1991

Published by Hodder and Stoughton,
a division of Hodder and Stoughton Ltd,
Mill Road, Dunton Green, Sevenoaks, Kent TN13 2YA.
Editorial Office: 47 Bedford Square, London WC1B 3DP.

Designed by Stocks Austin Sice,
2 Elgin Avenue, London W9 3QP

Typeset in Linotron Sabon and Gill Sans by
Rowland Phototypesetting Ltd, Bury St Edmunds, Suffolk

Printed in Great Britain by
St Edmundsbury Press Ltd, Bury St Edmunds, Suffolk

All profits from this book are being donated to Lloyd's Charities Trust, a fund established in 1953 in response to the growing number of appeals for charitable giving. The Trust now channels funds to more than 500 charities which cover a wide variety of activities. Projects supported range from local community initiatives in the East End of London to major national and international charities such as RNLI and Oxfam. The Trust is also on hand to provide funds to alleviate the effects of major disasters around the world.

CONTENTS

CONTENTS

· ·

H ave you noticed how obituaries have come back to life of late? No longer are they the ritual, pre-packed eulogies, as it were posthumous curtain-calls for the dead. Nowadays obituarists have licence to speak *bonum de mortuis* and anything else that made them interesting and, above all, human: their pretensions, prejudices, even their proclivities. And of course it all helps to sell newspapers too.

It was in this new spirit of freedom that this series of requiems was first conceived. After all, people are not the only things to pass away. Institutions wither and die as well, fashions fade, ways of life vanish, ideas are forgotten, species become extinct. Where are their memorials? Right here.

This series of valedictory essays began appearing in *Lloyd's Log*, the journal of Lloyd's of London, back in 1985 when the magazine was re-launched in its present form. It continues to appear, and over the years has produced a fascinating mixture of reminiscence and nostalgia, humour and pathos. This anthology is a selection of contributions over the past six years.

Our authors were invited to select their own corpse for interment. Together they are a powerful evocation of an era when people lived in lodgings rather than bed-sits, went on holidays to the seaside instead of Majorca, watched drawing-room comedies in place of 'Dallas', ate in tea rooms not in pizza parlours. Those were days when shop assistants in shops assisted you and bus-conductors took your fares; when courting was a rite of passage, and a real wedding the destination; when Soho had characters and Fleet Street journalists. Happy days. Or were they? See what you think.

Michael Wynn Jones

1

Recollections of Pastimes

NOW THE BALL IS OVER

T he other night, in a London theatre dressing-room, I met a lady
who had been born and raised in Dundee. Once upon a time
I had worked in that friendly town for several months, playing
the saxophone in a waterfront dance-hall. It was the time of 'Lavender
Blues' and 'My Foolish Heart' and 'Mona Lisa'. I was 22 years old and
living in a theatrical boarding house congested with dances from the local
variety theatre, and so naturally my memories of Dundee were fond ones.

"Tell me," I said to the lady in the dressing room, "how are things at the old Empress? Are they still taking the locks off the lavatory doors on Saturday nights?"

She looked at me in surprise, and said in that cute Angus twang, "Oh, but they knocked the Empress down years ago."

The news saddened me. I had spent some happy times within its walls, down there perched on the ragged fringes of the North Sea, with the stumps of the old Tay Bridge, McGonagall's bridge, still protruding from the water like the ends of blackened teeth. "I suppose, then," I replied, rallying bravely, "that the Locarno must be doing much better business now that the Empress is out of it."

"No," she said, "the Locarno's gone too."

"You mean that a town the size of Dundee is left with only the Palais as a dance-hall?"

"Not exactly," she said, "the Palais was shut down ages ago."

It is the same all over Britain. Although ballroom dancing survives, and although its devotees remain as fanatical as ever, and although a show like 'Come Dancing' survives as a television attraction for year after wearying year, the sad fact is that a whole way of nocturnal life is passing rapidly away. Before long the traditions will be forgotten, the rituals lost, the clichés fallen into disuse: "Do you come here often?", "Who's taking you home?", "Take your partners for an excuse-me fox-trot", "And now the spot prize". One night they will dismantle the last glitterball still in commission, that extraordinary device which brought a sort of romantic glow to so many millions of lives. For the benefit of those who have never lived beneath its shimmering spell, the glitterball is a hollow spheroid, about twice the size of a medicine ball, whose surface is made up of hundreds of pieces of small flat glass. When rotated from the ceiling while a single spotlight is trained upon it, the glitterball flings off a thousand blots of shadow gliding magically across the dance floor, dappling the faces of the dancers. A simple enough device, but one

which effectively blurs the distinctions between what is and what might
be.

My first dance-hall was Sherry's in Brighton, and I arrived there in
the summer of 1949 expecting to be corrupted by all sorts of delightful
sins. Like a great many others, I had been misled about Sherry's by
Graham Greene's comically lurid description of it in 'Brighton Rock'.
I had not worked in the place for two days before I realised that what
Greene had taken for scarlet sin was nothing more than scarlet electric
lamps running round the perimeter of the balcony. It was not sin which
distracted me but the dancers, who seemed to think that the number
of bars per minute were more important than the quality of the music,
and assumed that their ability to dance endowed them with infallible
musical judgment. From there I moved to a holiday camp where the
bandleader filled in the winter months working in a slaughterhouse.
And then to a Cambridge dance-hall whose tin roof turned into a set of
drums whenever heavy rain fell. After that the successive dance-halls
of my youth begin to blur into each other, a leaky bandroom here, a
paranoid ballroom manager there. But always the faces are the same,
shuffling round in an endless caucus race to the strains of the popular
airs of the moment. I measure my life, not in coffee spoons, but in hit songs,
'Teresa', 'Again', 'Slow Boat to China', 'Too Young', 'Be My Love',
'Smile', 'When I Fall in Love', and so on, world without apparent end.
And yet, if my informant from Dundee is right, the end has already come.

Although at the time I affected a deep contempt for the dance-hall
life, I have to acknowledge certain undeniable truths about strict-tempo
dancing which comprise an argument for its social importance. For one
thing, to go to a dance was the only way a young man could embrace a
strange woman without getting arrested. For another, it kept people off
the streets. And yet another, a musician, if he was subtle about it, could
practise his jazz arts without any of the dancers realising anything was
wrong. Britain today is filled with middle-aged couples who first met

during the Latin American medley, or first crashed into each other during the later rounds of 'The Hokey Cokey'. Had it not been for the dance-halls of old England, who knows where the marrieds of today would have found anyone willing to put up with them. What, for instance, of those folk who found romance in a certain Dublin dance-hall I played in back in 1954? Twenty-five years later the local television station got me to come back to the town and rediscover that ballroom. At last we found it, no longer a dance-hall but a room full of filing cabinets from the local hospital, who stocked all their terminal case histories there, and if that is not symbolic, I will eat my old Musicians' Union card.

I will never know now how many of my old work-places still stand, but the evidence seems to suggest that dance-halls are rather like synagogues in the East End of London, churches all over the place, Victorian football grounds, corner grocery shops, cats' meat men, coffee stalls, music-halls, picture palaces, doomed to disappear and be replaced by more up-to-date amenities. Naturally this makes me feel old, because it is my own past they are knocking down. Soon all that will be left will be memories, fond or otherwise. I think back and recall Wisbech Corn Exchange, where they used to sprinkle sand on the dance floor to camouflage evidence of recent cattle sales; the old Embassy at Cambridge, where the local American Air Force personnel used to come in laden with goods for sale from the PX; the Orange Grove somewhere near Birmingham, where one night our drummer got so carried away during his solo in 'Ole Man River' that one of the sticks flew out of his hand and hit a young lady flush on the nose; the Regent at Brighton, where you played at a great altitude because the ballroom was built on the top of the cinema; and Green's Playhouse in Glasgow, where one night the chaps stopped punching each other up on the balcony so that they could watch the girls punching each other; and Streatham Locarno, which I found so unbearable that one afternoon in mid-session I walked off the bandstand, went home and never came back, not even for my wages;

and Harpurhey Baths in Manchester, where some sailors got into a fight one night with the locals and were prevailed upon to stop when we gave them a hasty version of the national anthem, only to find that the moment the anthem was over the fight started up again where it had left off. And that hall in Welwyn Garden City where we got knocked for our fee. And the revolving stage at the Royal, Tottenham, which got stuck one night when we were halfway round. And that comical roughhouse of a place at Leith where, just before we arrived, Sean Connery was reputed to have been the bouncer. How many of these places have survived, or have their timbered floors been splintered by the developer's axe? Requiescat in Parquet. The age of live music is dead. Now is the winter of our discothèque.

CURTAIN RECALL

I greatly regret the complete disappearance from Shaftesbury Avenue and elsewhere of what used to be called 'drawing-room comedies', those untaxing dramatic offerings designed to display the talents of great female stars such as Marie Tempest and Lilian Braithwaite. They gladdened, particularly in the 1920s and 30s, my theatrical life. No school holiday was complete without at least one matinée outing with an indulgent parent or aunt in charge ("We're front row dress circle and we'll have tea in the second interval").

The plays took place, obviously, in drawing rooms and there was just one opulent set, the programme telling us that we were in 'Lady Bellamy's house in Belgravia Gardens. It is twelve-thirty on a sunny May morning'. Act II said 'Three weeks later', and Act III 'The following afternoon', adding that the curtain would be temporarily lowered 'to denote the passing of four hours'. It was the days of a programme note saying WILL LADIES KINDLY REMOVE THEIR HATS and, with this visual precaution safely accomplished, the house lights gradually lowered, the hum of conversation ("I see there's a sale on at Whiteley's") died away and we were off.

The curtain rose or, in the case of the Criterion Theatre, parted in the middle (if the Criterion one had gone upwards it would have emerged in Piccadilly Circus) and revealed a de luxe drawing room about which the programme's acknowledgments had already warned us – grand piano by Bechstein, silverware by Asprey, cigarettes by Abdullah, Miss Tempest's first act dress by Worth.

If the stage was empty the audience politely applauded the absent designer but in this imaginary case they do not do so for standing right centre is an extremely pretty parlourmaid answering the telephone and providing speech and plot which it is important we should hear. ". . . I really couldn't say, Madam . . . Her Ladyship telephoned from Harrods to say that she had been delayed . . . Yes, Madam, she is lunching in. We are expecting Miss Fairweather . . . Very good, Madam, I will inform her."

There now enters from down left, and presumably his study, Sir Theodore Bellamy, a handsome and dishevelled retired diplomat of 65 or so. He is patting his jacket pockets and looking puzzled. He speaks. "Ah, there you are, Alice. Be a good girl and help me to look for my spectacles. I had them only a moment ago . . ." Alice puts a hand to her mouth to repress a giggle and says: "Excuse me, sir, but I think you've got them on." He replies "Why, bless me, so I have. Goodness gracious, I shall be losing my head next," thus firmly establishing with the audience his well-loved character, that of a charming and bumbling old dear, teased by his wife and adored by all. Actors capable of sustaining this role were in those days two-a-penny.

Absent-mindedness always ranks high with audiences and during the delighted chuckle that follows a handsome young man enters from the double doors centre back and is clearly the son of the house. He gives Alice a playful pinch as he passes her and is greeted by his father with, "Ah there you are, Toby. Alice found my spectacles and now I can't remember where she said they were . . ." (he goes twittering off).

Alice then attempts to exit but is stopped by flirtatious Toby with, "Oh no you don't, my girl, not so fast," Alice countering strongly with, "Oh do give over, sir, I've got my job to consider." The front door bell rings loudly and, shortly after, a portly butler (he understudies Sir Theodore and is longing for him to break a leg or, preferably, die) announces "Miss Fairweather". Applause.

The English stage has always bristled with Miss Fairweathers, totally reliable actresses who are not quite stars but are always high up in the billing, as it might be Marda Vanne or Martita Hunt. They play the female star's best friend. They smoke, they are well dressed, and they play toughish and no-nonsense spinsters. Indeed, on this occasion Miss Fairweather's opening lines are "What the hell is your mother up to, Toby? She rang me at God knows what early hour and insisted I came to lunch. Don't say that she's dreamt up yet another crack-brained scheme for making money! Here, give me a cigarette, and do you think that Merrydew could rustle me up a White Lady?"

Sir Theodore reappears, says, "Ah, there you are, Grace. Stella said you were coming. I'm a bit worried about her. She's been looking very odd recently. I do hope that we're not in for . . ." His voice dies away for a car is heard stopping, the front door bangs, the audience buzzes with excitement and an unmistakable voice tells Merrydew to take all the cardboard boxes up to her room. It is Marie Tempest, a magical presence and the reason why we are here. Those of us who saw her are for ever blessed, for this particular type of actress exists no more, and just as well for there are now no plays for her.

There is a storm of applause while Miss Tempest rearranges the flowers on the piano and, a favourite trick, runs her finger along the top to test for dust and finding some, raises her eyebrows and achieves a chuckle. Sir Theodore says, as expected, "Ah, there you are, Stella. What are you up to, my dear?" and off Miss Tempest goes, teasing, bantering, being secretive and roguish until Merrydew enters and says "Luncheon is served m'lady". Upon which, Stella moves centre stage and says, "All right. I'll tell you so that you can enjoy your lunch. You mustn't call me Stella anymore, Theo. From now on I'm Estelle. I'M GOING TO OPEN A HAT SHOP!" "Where, for God's sake?" shouts her husband. "Why, here of course!" Quick curtain.

There then followed what was called in the text, TABLEAU. The curtain rose at once to reveal, all motionless, Sir Theodore collapsed on the sofa with mouth open in astonishment and horror, Toby with his head in hands, Grace shaking an admonitory finger at Stella, Merrydew with his eyes raised to heaven, and Miss Tempest looking, centre back, triumphant.

Lovely! Our hands were raw with clapping.

PASSING OF THE DREAM PALACE

I went to the cinema the other evening. Well, it makes a change from haunting the local video shop where lovers of the art queue up to rent uncensored copies of 'The Texas Chainsaw Massacre' and 'Behind Convent Walls'. But it was a dispiriting occasion. The box office was next to a fast-food counter where there was a choice between popcorn in plastic tubs and hot dogs striped with tomato ketchup the colour of rust. There were not many takers, but the detritus on the floor showed

11

that business had been brisk. Someone had been sick in the centre aisle and a senior citizen left over from the cut-price matinée was either dead or asleep in the stalls. Welcome to the Pleasure Dome.

Something awful has happened to the British cinema – the bricks and mortar, I mean, rather than what's shown there. The dream palace has gone and it is a loss which I take personally. Since the age of four when my mother took me to see what was perhaps the last of the great silent westerns, James Cruze's 'The Covered Wagon', I have been a film addict. For a while I was able to rationalise my addiction by becoming a film critic. But it's not only the art which claims me. It is the plush darkness in which all things are possible. For the best part of 50 years the cinema has been my second home, an entire gamut of second homes, in fact, ranging from the passion pits of my adolescence where the back row beneath the balcony featured large settees for courting couples to the art house in Los Angeles where the air conditioning was so ferocious that huskies rather than usherettes were needed to show you to your seat.

They all had their charms. I remember an open-air cinema in Cairo which was showing a World War II drama in which an Allied patrol anxiously scanned the skies, looking for the plane which would bring them aid. Mysteriously, they failed to see it, clearly silhouetted at the top right-hand corner of the screen. But then the shape scuttled sideways and we realised that the action had been invaded by a lizard, stalking moths in the glare of the projector. The performance, I remember, became very much a social occasion. The lights went up several times and waiters dispensed Coca-Cola and mint tea. No one worried too much about the lost patrol, but the togetherness was terrific.

All the same, it was not serious movie-going and the purist in me disapproved. I have always felt that going to the cinema was something special. Cinemas themselves were the temples of the Thirties and Forties, the decades in which I lost my religious faith and found another. I was brought up in the Potteries, a district celebrated by Arnold Bennett as the Five Towns, although there were really six, and each of them had at least two picture-houses. There was the Regent, the Palace, the Coliseum (a former theatre with pillars still intact which regulars took care to avoid), the Roxy, the Globe, the Ritz, the Empire and the Palladium.

The Regent was the posh one. There were deep monogrammed carpets leading through doors of frosted glass and softly-lit portraits of the stars lined the walls of the restaurant. Afternoon teas with potted-meat sandwiches and fairy cakes were served by waitresses wearing starched white crowns.

"They always do you well there," my mother used to say, as though what you paid for and what you got was ordained by a social contract more profound than any cash transaction. The manager wore a dinner jacket, only a trifle frayed, and bowed from the waist to regular patrons. The disinfectant, sprayed discreetly before the first house, smelled of pine forests. And the organist, when he ascended from his pit in a glass chariot whose walls glowed rose and pistachio, made celestial music. At the Regent, picture-palace extraordinary, they ministered to the soul as well as the body.

Usually we were taken there by adults, but on our own we went to the Palladium. It was in a small mining village in a street at whose end a tip – a man-made mountain of colliery waste – poked up like a sleeping volcano. Inside the cinema it was curious to think of it standing sentinel, a reminder that whatever the Palladium offered by way of escape, there was still work to be done.

They had rats there, everybody warned us. Why else would they maintain a corps of cats – black, tabby and tortoiseshell – to patrol the aisles, slinking under the tip-up seats, brushing our legs when the lights went out? They had other things too. To our parents, the Palladium was 'the bug-hutch' and our visits there were not encouraged. We ignored the warnings. Of course the Palladium was a disgrace. The projection jumped like a torch in the hand of a drunken man, paper darts planed

13

down from the gallery and peanut shells detonated under foot like small-arms fire. It was every bit as bad as they said. And we loved it.

The Palladium punctuated my life with holidays. It was where I liked to be best, anonymous in the dark, horsehair oozing from the upholstery and pricking my bare thighs, a Victory lozenge fuming in my mouth and on the screen Errol Flynn setting torch to the Spanish Main or Charlie Chase on a bicycle gone berserk. At the Palladium I saw 'Flash Gordon on the Planet Mars' and 'The Haunted Mine' starring Tim McCoy, a sharp-shooting buckaroo and real-life army colonel, whose white stetson curled like an aristo's lip. I saw Laurel and Hardy and The Three Stooges and Rin-Tin-Tin the Wonder Dog and Jimmy Durante and Shirley Temple tapping step for step with the great Bill Robinson and all for threepence admission, with a bag of boiled sweets, an apple and an orange thrown in on Saturday afternoons.

I read recently of a new complex that was being built at, I think, Milton Keynes, which would house eight cinemas, a restaurant and a bar under one roof. The idea, said the report, was to bring back the family audience and I applaud the intention. Anything would be better than the hot-dog stand with the screen attached that I suffered the other night. But more than hygiene, more than salesmanship is needed to make it a success. Something in the air, perhaps; a measure of plush darkness, distilled four decades ago and bottled with love. Between the commercials and the coming attractions is there anybody listening?

. . . .

A LONG WAVE GOODBYE

F or the first twelve years of my life I lived in a house with neither electricity nor bathroom. The front parlour was for Christmas, entertaining visitors, piano practice and the aspidistra, while in the back room on a shelf next to the fire, pride of place was reserved for the box of spare gas mantles and the wireless.

It wasn't a proper wireless of course. The absence of mains electricity obliged my parents to pay weekly for broadcasts piped into a simple loudspeaker from the nearest town. The choice of programmes depended on the whim of the controller at the Radio Relays office two miles away who could be depended on to switch over from the Home Service to the Third just before the end of 'Saturday Night Theatre' when the villain would be unmasked. I would then wonder why, since science had managed to come up with the gas-powered refrigerator, it was unable to do something similar for the reception of radio waves. I still do not know who murdered Roger Ackroyd.

The wireless was strong magic. It filled my head with vivid, technicolour pictures, taught me more than I ever learned at school and gave my life a reassuringly regular pattern. On Tuesday evenings the zinc bathtub was taken down from its hook on the wall opposite the scullery window, water boiled in kettles and saucepans on the stove and I was given my bath in front of the fire, accompanied by 'In Town Tonight' on the wireless. On Saturday mornings the omnibus edition of 'Dick Barton' would take me to Limehouse, Mayfair or the Yorkshire Moors as Dick, Jock and Snowy saved the free world from yet another international conspiracy. On Sundays lunch was accompanied by another kind of feast: 'Educating Archie', 'Ray's a Laugh' or 'Life with the Lyons'. Only a Trappist monk listening to a reading from 'The Imitation of Christ' while he dines could imagine such exquisite pleasure.

My early life revolved around the wireless and mostly what was then the Home Service. But there was also Radio Luxembourg – 208 metres on the medium wave – which, apart from the hilarity unwittingly provided by Horace Batchelor of Keynsham advertising his pools-winning Infradraw Method and a record-request programme called 'It's My Mother's Birthday' introduced by Godfrey Wynne, also broadcast 'Dan Dare, Pilot of the Future' (sponsored by Horlicks) nightly from Monday to Friday. It was almost as good as the comic strip in *The Eagle*. One

unforgettable evening in February 1952 an eagerly awaited episode was postponed to make way for hours of solemn, uninterrupted music. It was years before I forgave King George VI for dying on a weekday.

When I went away to school I was homesick more for the wireless than for home itself and immediately set about constructing a one-valve receiver – not because I was fascinated by the technology but simply because I wanted to listen through army surplus headphones to 'PC49' or 'Book at Bedtime' after the others in the dormitory had gone to sleep. All my pocket money went on condensers, resistors, capacitors and an aerial – 100 yards of insulating wire meandering from tree to tree which, depending on sunspots or the Heaviside layer, could sometimes pull in the American Forces Network from Frankfurt, Germany.

There was one sophisticated wireless on the premises. It stood in what was hopefully called The Quiet Room which only lived up to its name once a week when the latest episode of 'Journey into Space' was broadcast. Then even the house bully sat transfixed by the sound of airlocks opening and closing. They did this with a frequency which increased as the scriptwriter ran out of ideas for the plot.

By then radio (as we had come to call it) had begun to relax its grip on my imagination. 'Dick Barton' made way for 'The Archers' while such Children's Hour perennials as 'Jennings at School' and 'Norman and Henry Bones, Boy Detectives', slowly lost their power to amuse and excite. This wasn't entirely radio's fault, more the inevitable result of the advent of both adolescence and television. My parents had moved to a house with electricity and a TV set and I now longed for home and regular instalments of 'I Married Joan' and 'Highway Patrol'. How could Ambridge compete with California?

I know that I'm not so much lamenting the decline of the wireless here as mourning a much graver loss: nothing less than that of childhood and innocence. It's unlikely that anything broadcast 40 years ago was truly as good, or that today's radio is really as disappointing as memory makes it seem.

But am I just imagining that there used to be much more talk – marvellous, stimulating talk – on Radio 3 when it was still the Third Programme? Am I alone in wondering why there needs to be 90 minutes of news and weather forecasts on Radio 4 between 5.00 and 6.30 p.m., and why the only guests on 'Start the Week' are people with books to plug? And must all local stations from Cumbria to Cornwall play the same pop records introduced by disc jockeys with the same fake American accents?

Whenever I find myself listening to the terminal bores on 'Any Questions' or yet another 'phone-in', I am persuaded to think that my gilded recollections of the great days of steam radio may not be as misleading as all that. And if there hasn't been a decline at least in the standard of comedy programmes, why does the BBC transmit so many repeats of 'Round the Horne' and 'Hancock's Half Hour'? In fairness, however, I must admit that even they don't make me laugh as loudly the ninth and tenth time around. I cannot bear to think how much 'In Town Tonight' might disappoint me if those tapes were now resurrected from the archives – unless, that is, that magisterial voice stopping the mighty roar of London's traffic could once again be heard from a simple Radio Relays loudspeaker while I wallow in a zinc bathtub in front of the fire.

MERCIFUL RELEASES

'The British musical, as we knew it, passed away in 1956 after a series of illnesses which had seemed likely to prove fatal. Even after the death the corpse twitched eerily for several years, although it had been pronounced extinct.' That announcement might well have appeared in the obituary column of the *Stage* newspaper, a faithful recorder of the vagaries of British musical taste. First nights of post-war shows were a fascinating lottery – partly because a dangerous animal was at large in the theatre, the gallery. I cannot now remember the last time I heard the ugly sound of a gallery baying: but through the Fifties and Sixties it was often in full cry and the musical was the art form that brought out the worst in it.

The first musical to incur the wrath of the gallery after the war was a vehicle for Cicely Courtneidge called 'Her Excellency'. Kurt Ganzl, the definitive historian of British musical theatre, reports that 'the danger signs were there on the first night. An audience come to welcome Miss Courtneidge back to London heard her given the slow handclap. Most of the show had been negotiated before the star came forward to give her principal number, a sentimental piece, 'Sunday Morning in England' ... It was the type of thing she did particularly well but it was not easy to cut and change the mood from the heartfelt to the mischievous and back and successfully hold the audience. On the first night the gallery was not held and the demonstration began. The bulk of the audience was duly indignant and applauded their favourite all the more.'

It was a pattern that was to be repeated many times in the following years. 'Her Excellency' had the usual silly plot (ambassadress to a South American republic can't make up her romantic mind between the American ambassador and a dago meat king). At least five creative hands assembled the concoction which was hacked and patched in its uncertain progress around the provinces on its journey to the West End.

In the same season Bobby Howes and Pat Kirkwood were soundly booed in an even soppier vehicle called 'Roundabout' which lasted only 27 performances. The next year the great Noel Coward suffered the indignity of a rowdy gallery at the first night of his modest Soho musical 'Ace of Clubs'. I imagine it was the first time they had given him 'the bird' since the disastrous opening of his much earlier play 'Sirocco' in the Twenties.

But it is 1955 and 1956 that I remember as particularly rich in awful shows. British confidence had been sapped by the post-war American invasion: 'Oklahoma', 'Annie Get Your Gun', 'Brigadoon' and 'Kiss Me Kate' had destroyed homegrown optimism. 'The Boyfriend' was a solitary spark of indigenous enlightenment to be followed in 1954 by 'Salad Days'.

But 1955 and 1956 were something else in awfulness. I remember going to the first 1955 offering at the Royal Court – very much before the English Stage Company's regime began. In fact I went to two first nights that evening – the only time I have done it. At the earlier showing of a Teddy Boy melodrama playing twice nightly at the Chelsea Palace in repertoire with 'The Sign of the Cross' and 'East Lynne', I saw the first half and then proceeded down the King's Road to Sloane Square for a very curious concoction called 'The Burning Boat' which had something to do with primitive passions and a highbrow music festival in a fishing village. I sat in the front row and my most vivid memory is the first-half finale in which the small cast skipped round in a circle singing a repetitive refrain, 'Dancing and turning round the burning boat!' while the veteran actress Marie Ney could be clearly heard saying loudly, "Oh dear, I'm absolutely lost but it's such fun!"

The Players' Theatre produced a modest success 'Twenty Minutes South' – a suburban commuter musical – but the next abject disaster was a quaint whimsy called 'Wilde Thyme' with a wonderfully eccentric set by the ingenious cartoonist Ronald Searle. However *The Times* found some merit in it and pronounced: 'This country frolic is as innocent as a daisy and as fresh as a buttercup.' It was also about as exciting as watching grass grow.

Worse was to follow – not necessarily in 'The Water Gipsies', a flat evening which found A. P. Herbert and Vivian Ellis below their best form in a river barge musical which only an exuberant performance by Dora Bryan saved from sinking – but emphatically in 'Candlelight', an

21

incredibly turgid piece of nonsense based on a German play from the Twenties which sputtered for a couple of weeks at the Piccadilly.

Not one but two adaptations of Tom Robertson's Victorian play 'Caste' surfaced in the provinces, one at Windsor, the other at Worthing. The Worthing offering got to the West End first under a new title, 'She Smiled at Me'. I saw it on the Friday at the St Martin's Theatre – which was about halfway through its run of four performances. Mr Ganzl, who had inside knowledge, reports that when the impresario Melville Gillam posted the closing notice on the Saturday night his star pleaded, "Oh, don't put up the notice!" to which he replied, "I'd have put it up sooner if I'd had the time."

Worse was to come in 1956. 'Wild Grows the Heather', a ponderous adaptation of Barrie's 'Little Minister', lasted 27 performances at the London Hippodrome. After a reasonably successful first act Val Parnell, who ran the Hippodrome, turned down substantial agency offers for ticket advances to be confronted by a disastrous second act which dissipated everyone's desire to buy any tickets at all. 'Jubilee Girl', composed and backed by a wealthy Marks & Spencer son-in-law, had seven changes of director and choreographer on its way to London and only one of the original six featured players, Fenella Fielding, made it to the stage of the Victoria Palace.

The most extravagant flop, 'The Crystal Heart', was not technically a British musical. It had American authors but an emphatically English cast. Its tour had started disastrously in Scotland when a tray of real glass glasses had been dropped on the stage just before a barefoot sailor's ballet. The London opening was worse. Hisses and boos and slow handclaps punctuated the proceedings until Gladys Cooper was called upon to gaze aloft and cry "The Bird! The Bird!" Whereupon the gallery gave it to her.

22   On it went through the Fifties and Sixties with John Osborne's 'World

of Paul Slickey' howled out of the Palace Theatre and Lionel Bart's 'Twang' screamed off the stage of the Prince's.

It's all quieter now and the Lloyd Webber machine and Cameron Macintosh's experienced professionalism have done much to take the risk factor out of big musicals. So I regret the passing of the laughably awful show and the bear baiting mood of the gallery. I shouldn't; but a nagging voice tells me I might be kidding myself.

· ·

When the 'season of goodwill' is over, how many letters do you receive, I wonder. Not the perfunctory greeting scrawled on a belated Christmas card – 'We really must meet in the New Year' – not the obligatory 'bread and butter' letter from someone who had to be sent a token present though you scarcely know them. Above all, I am not referring to the chirpy tape sent by a child whose parents assume that you will be thrilled by the sound of the piping voice. Of course a tape is easier than writing a letter, and that is part of the trouble. It holds as much romance as a fax.

Hand-written letters require a certain effort which most people are not prepared to give nowadays when so many machines demand their attention. I am one of a vanishing breed, regarding letter-writing as a pleasure rather than a duty, and sufficiently old-fashioned to abhor the fax and word processor.

Prince Charles has declared that 'ours is the age of miraculous writing machines but not of miraculous writing', but all I lament is the simple grace of keeping people in touch through letters which offer a sympathy denied by the telephone. Anyone who has waited outside a phone box or stumbled on a crossed-line will recognise the grunts, repetitions, silences and utter triviality of the conversation overheard – the interminable platitudes of other people: 'um . . . yes, lovely . . . brilliant . . . cold with you, is it? yes . . . I've got to go, Maureen, I'll ring this evening, when it's cheaper . . . yes . . . well, bye for now . . . cheerio . . . bye-bye . . . bye' as if they cannot bear to lay the receiver to rest.

In contrast, the letter dares not afford such self-indulgence, demanding a clarity and crispness which prompts the well-known quip – 'sorry it's such a long letter, I haven't the time to write you a short one'.

I am not extolling letter-writing as an art, cringing from the pretentiousness of the correspondence conducted by two intellectuals who point their *bons mots* like darts, with the hope that their witty literary illusions will end up in book form. The man who is writing for posterity is writing for himself, whereas the true letter-writer conveys feelings which may seem awkward when expressed aloud but are perfectly acceptable on the page. This is why a letter has more spontaneity than a calculated diary.

Literacy is not the prerequisite. When I was in the army, yielding as always to my curiosity, I salvaged some crumpled pages of a love-letter

written by a soldier who had struggled for hours to find the right words
for his girlfriend, but the sentiment rang true and that is what mattered.

Love-letters! Do people still write them today, or tie them up in
bundles with pink ribbons to be treasured for years in a locked box or the
back of a private drawer, to be taken out years later as evidence of
something young and wonderful? I hope so, for I am incurably
romantic, yet I doubt it. Time, or the shortage of it, prevents such chivalry
now that we have so many things to do today, like watching television.

The Victorians, who were spared this flickering vampire, regarded
letter-writing as a natural grace, all the more so in the knowledge that
a letter posted in London in the morning would be delivered that evening
on the other side of town. With time on their side, they used it for
painting watercolours, reading aloud, needlework and the courtesy of
letters for every occasion, from birth to the black-edged notepaper of
mourning. Ironically, death is still the occasion when people resort to
letters of commiseration, though the hardest to write.

Victorian men cultivated friendship with a warmth which was
innocent though unthinkable now. In his capacity as manager of the Lyceum
Theatre, my great-uncle, Bram Stoker, wrote 200 to 300 hundred letters
a week, and many of these were personal. Given a sack of such letters
by his son, I discovered a message scribbled in pencil from Sir Henry
Irving, stating: 'You, of all men, whom I hold dear'; and another from
Oscar Wilde who wrote emotionally to Ellen Terry on a first night asking
her to give a crown of lilies to my great-aunt Florence, who had jilted
him for Bram: 'Don't think me treacherous, Nellie – but the other (crown)
please give to Florrie as from yourself. I should like to think she was wearing
something of mine . . . that anything of mine should touch her. Of course
if you think – but you won't think she will suspect? How could she? She
thinks I never loved her, thinks I forgot. My God how could I?'
Conversely, my grandfather, Tom Stoker, was meticulously stiff and

proper even while courting my grandmother, signing his letters with his surname, though he waxed more eloquently after his proposal: 'Please let me know what you decide – by a wire unless there is time to write. Good night dearest – I am so sleepy – I suppose from the ride – I am off to bed in hopes I may dream of She. Ye Ever loving, Tom.'

Plainly, letter-writing was a family tradition, and my grandmother wrote so many letters to her sisters, in spite of living into the age of the telephone, that one of them became a family joke: 'As I write this I can see your taxi turning round the corner, but I felt I had to write to say how much . . .'

My mother maintained it at the age of 18, when she sailed for St Petersburg as a VAD nurse in 1916. Her accounts from the Anglo-Russian hospital owned by the Grand Duke Dimitri Pavelitch have a period interest today, such as the visit from the Tsarina: 'The two little princesses, Olga and Tatiana, looked charming and so pretty in little ermine hats and white ospreys on them and low-necked rose-coloured frocks and ermine furs and muffs. Olga is the prettiest and really lovely I thought and all so jolly-looking and natural. All our Embassy were there in full fig and all the Secretaries and Attachés we used to dance with made us roar – all covered in gold lace and things.' She described how the Grand Duke Dimitri burst in at dawn with Prince Yussipov, blood-stained and apparently drunk until the doctors realised they were in a state of hysteria. They had just killed Rasputin. At the same time, my father, the American writer Negley-Farson, who was selling munitions to the corrupt Tsarist regime, was shown the claw marks on the frozen River Neva where Rasputin tried to crawl out after being poisoned and shot.

There is another, before me now, which I find infinitely touching, from my great-grandmother, in her nineties, to my grandmother: 'My own darling Dormouse, I wish you very very many happy returns on your birthday and I send you the enclosed cheque in the *entre toi et moi* envelope with so much love. I cannot tell you how much I love you or how much I thank God for giving me such a dear daughter . . . I respect and admire you for the good life you try to live day in day out in good times and bad times . . . You mean such a lot in my life and I love you so near.' That is the delight of this simple letter: she lived on the corner at 15 Pelham Crescent and could wave to my grandmother across the road in Pelham Place. They were bound to meet each other later that day, but this was a personal bond between them alone.

Perhaps I am ridiculous to mourn the loss of letter-writing, but I feel that one of the more charming attributes of life has gone.

LOVE IN THE AFTERNOON

They're gone now; like foggy days, empty roads and Lyon's Corner Houses, but somewhere they must still lie in waiting, their once-shining containers dulled by the passing years, ready to be excavated by an unborn generation of cinema archaeologists. The lost genre of British B Films.

In the 50s they were as much part of our adolescent lives as music by Frankie Laine, drugs by Wild Woodbines and sex made safe by the grave courtesy of a white-coated barber ("Anything else, sir?" they would intone as they brushed the tiny hairs from your shoulders and down the neck of your shirt.) Sunday afternoons were our time, when the only movement on the wet shuttered high streets came from the jostling lines of impatient youths waiting in eager anticipation for the cinemas to open for business.

Hollywood usually provided the big feature and for us, whose only inheritance were the picture palaces of the 30s, the glittering streets of New York and pitiless deserts of Arizona seemed far more real than the Elizabethan manor houses, svelte London flats and seedy Soho nightclubs where the action of British B films were set.

The main feature sometimes held our attention, at least until a particularly demanding passage of dialogue took place on the screen, then a roar of conversation would rise from most sections of the cinema, like the chant of a Zulu army that was about to attack and would only be subdued by subsequent scenes of violent action.

The seating arrangements on these occasions conformed to a hierarchical code as rigid as the Samurai traditions of ancient Japan. The cheapest rows were where the youngest roamed, I use the term advisedly, as their seething masses rarely remained seated for more than thirty seconds at a time. Sex was not important to those pre-adolescent mobs: scuffles, practical jokes and vulgar observations during the love scenes were their forte.

Parts of the broad block behind them were equally mobile, but for other reasons. Hoping to employ the equipment supplied by our friendly barbers, we questing youths would execute a series of moves complex enough to cause envy in the heart of a chess master, as we battled to place ourselves close to the girls we desired.

The girls never moved. Paired by natural selection into the pretty and the plain, they would be stalked in the flickering darkness until rejection or selection had taken place. Those of us who were lucky enough to find romance might well be elevated to the back rows on our next visit, which were reserved by common consent for those who had formed passionate partnerships. Once there, we would lock mouth to mouth and attempt to progress the relationship by caressing a breast shaped like a pyramid encased in wire and padded satin.

The dress circle was left to engaged couples who had done their time in the hurly-burly below and had now graduated to the cosy intimacy of holding hands over a box of Black Magic. Sometimes, if we had failed to find a suitable partner, we lone youths were forced by boredom to actually watch parts of the second feature.

Now, when I look back, they all seem to have merged into the same film. It would begin with Paul Carpenter arriving in England carrying a nylon holdall which instantly established him as a North American. (British people always carried cardboard suitcases.) He would book into a country hotel, where the following dialogue would take place.

DESK CLERK: Mr Conway, from Toronto. Would you be an American, sir?

CARPENTER: No Canadian. I'm looking up an old war-time buddy of mine who lives around here. He used to be my rear-gunner. You may know him, Chalky White?

DESK CLERK: You might try up at the Hall, sir. Chalky White's late father was gardener to Lord Bathwater.

Paul Carpenter would take a taxi to the Hall, where Lord Bathwater's daughter, a graduate from the Rank Starlet Academy, greeted him with the sort of vowel sounds Eliza Doolittle would have killed for.

They would fall in love instantly and set off together having learned from the kitchen maid that Chalky had been framed in a stolen car racket, lost the garage he had bought with his savings and set off to take personal revenge on the guilty gang leader.

Once in London, the couple would find out that Mr Big, played by David Farrar, owned a night club called the Blue Parrot, managed by

31

an actor called Denis Shaw, who had a face like a puzzled toad and always wore a dinner-jacket, even at ten o'clock in the morning.

Paul Carpenter would confront Shaw and a fight would take place that knocked the Blue Parrot's wobbly scenery about a bit. Then Roland Culver would appear as a police inspector, wearing a riding mac and a racing trilby, as if he were on his way to a point-to-point. He would take them back to Scotland Yard where he would warn Carpenter to keep out of police business.

But having found a clue that Chalky was being held prisoner at Walton-on-Thames, they would ignore the warning and head up river, arriving just as Mr Big was leaving for the Continent aboard his motor cruiser, leaving Chalky chained to a mooring post in anticipation of high tide.

Miss Rank would release him from the boathouse while Carpenter tackled Mr Big. Carpenter would win the exchange of blows but Mr Big would produce a gun and fire wildly. Carpenter would dive overboard just as one of the random shots hit the petrol tank, thus incinerating Mr Big, polluting a quiet backwater of the Thames, restoring Chalky's ownership of the garage business and leaving Paul Carpenter to enjoy a lifetime of elocution lessons.

Rubbish? Certainly. Entertainment value? Zero. But remember, America produced B movies in the 40s that French film critics elevated to the status of an art form, calling the genre: film noir. So who knows what could happen to their British counterparts. They're almost bad enough to show on television now and after all, they did teach my generation how to love.

· ·

2

Dead March of Progress

THE NUMBER'S UP

I n a Bishopsgate call-box in 1907 Mr Samuel Wartski, enraged
because the operator had not heard him inserting his coins and
refused to connect him, produced a chisel and attacked the coinbox
in an attempt to retrieve his tuppence. The box held out, Mr Wartski
was arrested and in due course he was fined a shilling with two guineas
costs. He then disappeared into obscurity, not realising perhaps that he had
created for himself a special niche in Britain's social history. He was our

first telephone vandal. Mr Wartski's successors have been smashing up phone boxes on a fairly regular basis ever since, and it is largely because of their activities that the most famous phone box of all, Sir Giles Gilbert Scott's K6, was adjudged too vulnerable to vandals and received the death sentence.

Most non-vandals, however, have rather an affection for these sturdy red boxes which have been part of our daily lives for so long. It is sad to see them facing the ignominy of becoming mini-bars or shower cabinets or very small conservatories. They have been as much an emblem of the British way of life to overseas visitors as Big Ben, Changing the Guard, and warm beer. Their story must not be forgotten – Wartskis and all.

A hundred years ago each rival telephone company was designing its own style of call-box, ranging from rustic arbours to converted workmen's huts. Blackburn installed in its roomy kiosk not only a telephone but comfortable seats and a table. The latter were removed after four gentlemen of no fixed abode were discovered enjoying a quiet game of cards. But most kiosks just had a coinbox, or a coin-operated door, or an attendant who took the money and stood outside while the call was made. One hopes he was supplied with a company umbrella.

When the Post Office took over the telephone network in 1912 it decided to have a standard kiosk for the whole country. Nine years later it produced one – a rather charming affair with a lot of windows, some fancy wrought-iron work, and a spear sticking out of the roof. Dr Who might have christened it the Spiked Tardis. The Post Office, more cautiously, called it the K1. It failed to catch on. People had grown fond of their wooden sheds and rustic arbours, and city councils did not want any more phone boxes anyway – they regarded them more as a traffic hazard than a public amenity. So the Post Office decided to tempt them with something a little more up-market. It held a competition

35

among three leading architects and Sir Giles Gilbert Scott produced the
K2.

Sir Giles had already designed Liverpool's Anglican Cathedral and
later he was to design Battersea Power Station, but in 1925 he was
concentrating on kiosks. He produced a cast-iron model with a teak door
and a concrete base, small window panes and a curved roof. It was, with
some modification, the red kiosk we have grown to know so well.
Architects liked it because of its classical lines. The Post Office liked it
because it seemed difficult to damage. Customers liked it because it was
rain-proof, draught-proof and very nearly sound-proof. Town councils
liked it because it matched its urban surroundings. Only some rural areas
continued to oppose it, plus a few places like Eastbourne which had put
thatched roofs on its kiosks and kept them like that until the 1930s. One
critic observed that they looked like a cross between a Chinese pagoda and
a mushroom.

As the K2 began to appear on the nation's street corners Sir Giles and
the Post Office did not rest on their kiosks. Sir Giles switched from
cast-iron to concrete for the K3, but it was difficult to transport without
bits breaking off and if it did arrive in one piece the British weather cracked
the concrete and blistered the paint. Several thousand were made but
only a handful survive. Meanwhile the Post Office Engineering
Department had a go themselves. They took the K2 and added a
miniature post office on one side of it. They installed a couple of stamp
machines and a letter-box, and above them, on Sir Giles's classical roof,
they stuck a lamp.

Nobody liked the Vermillion Giants, as they came to be known. They
were so bulky they blocked the pavement, telephone users were
inconvenienced by the noise from the stamp machines, and the rolls of
stamps got damp and stuck together. Only fifty were made before the
project was abandoned. One or two still exist, bright red reminders of
all those bright red faces in the Engineering Department. But they did

not give up. They produced the K5, which was so unsatisfactory it never reached the public. Sir Giles came to the rescue with his K6, a lighter, smaller version of the K2, with wider window-panes to improve visibility, less decorative fluting, and ventilation through slots under the 'Telephone' sign instead of holes in the ornamental crown on the roof. It was equipped with the new 'Button B' coinboxes.

That was in 1935, the year of King George's silver jubilee, and they called it the Jubilee Kiosk. It went forth and multiplied, and when Sir Giles died in 1960 there were 60,000 of them. On city streets and village greens, on top of Welsh mountains and alongside Scottish lochs, by busy beaches or on lonely moors, next to a London office block or up a Cornish cliff – the red box was there. And so, alas, were the latter-day Wartskis. In the 1960s, on average, every kiosk in Britain was being vandalised twice a year. The Post Office produced a K7, which was not a success, and a K8, which was. It had big windows to reveal what was going on inside, gaps under the walls so rubbish did not accumulate, tougher fixtures and fittings. If one can imagine the traditional red box having a coffin, the K8 was the first nail in it.

In 1984 British Telecom was born, and ordered the interment. It announced that all Scott's kiosks would be replaced, not by a K9 – Dr Who's canine robot would have enjoyed that confusion – but by an assortment of kiosks, semi-kiosks, booths and head-canopies, based on American and Continental designs. They would no longer be Post Office red but Telecom yellow.

Since then 30,000 Scott kiosks have been replaced, and the purge continues. Just a couple of thousand will be allowed to survive as 'listed buildings'. Others have become garden ornaments, on a par with fake wishing wells and garden gnomes. I have heard of one which is being converted into a loo. The rest are rusting away in scrapyards, the saddest sight of all. Gavin Stamp, chairman of the Thirties Society and chief mourner for the Scott kiosks, wrote of this doomed species: 'They were

37

not only admirable and efficient as weathertight receptacles for public telephones, they were also supremely excellent models of how sensitive, dignified and, yes, beautiful street furniture can be.' Which is pushing it a bit, but Amen anyway.

TYPEWRITING ON THE WALL

began to lose interest in pens at the age of twelve, when I was disqualified from a handwriting competition for submitting my entry in biro. In vain did I protest that it was a Coronation biro with a crown on top – as officially dispensed to all schoolchildren – and presumably had the royal imprimatur. My antipathy subsequently deepened during the recurring transcription of 'lines', one of the most curious and futile punishments known to Man. Only when I was bequeathed a typewriter by an aged relative, though, did I fully realise the extent of my bondage to permanent ink and blotting pads.

It was an antediluvian, sit-up-and-beg Remington, but it gave a palpable power to words. Portable it was not; it was immovable. The pistol-crack of the typebars and the juddering recoil of the carriage reminded you forcibly of the fact that Remington had originally been a gunsmith. When those keys crunched the words on to paper, they stayed written. The old monster had one endearing quirk however: fitted up with a two-colour ribbon, it printed every letter half-black and half-red. No amount of shuffling with the little gearstick would alter its aesthetics.

I learned one thing very quickly with my Remington, which was that I could never hope to retype an article in fair copy before paralysis of the fingers set in. I guess that is why, even now, I prefer to stare for hours at a blank sheet of paper rather than commit myself to a sentence I might have to retype.

My next machine could not have been more different, a dainty almost effete Olivetti portable, and we established a very close relationship. She was a symbol of my new profession of journalist: have typewriter, will travel. I reckon she must have logged several hundred flying hours, her bakelite case getting more and more chipped, her handle finally hanging on one hinge. She once travelled all on her own on a Greyhound bus from Chicago to Des Moines, faithfully guarding a seat to which I failed to return. She was once impounded, and interrogated for all I know, for several hours by a customs official in Khartoum. I paid the ransom, of course.

We always got back together again, but she would show her wilfulness in a variety of ways, most often by discarding the letter N from her vocabulary – making it impossible for me to type my name with any conviction. On such occasions we would repair to an Irishman called Sean who conducted a typewriter surgery in a garden shed in Camden. In this ramshackle workshop, pungent with oil and ink, Sean would solder the errant letter back on at any time of the day or night, endlessly extolling the virtues of old-fashioned platens, or execrating some new-fangled linkage system. I knew his time had come when they introduced revolving golf-balls, so I don't think I was too surprised when one evening we found the shed shuttered and a notice on the door to the effect that Sean had gone to meet a deadline with his Dictator.

The letter N never did get soldered back on again, and the little old lady went into graceful retirement. I flirted uneasily with a number of successors before settling down with an electric Smith-Corona, which gave cute little electronic peeps of encouragement at the end of every line, as if to say so far so good, give me more. It even had a memory. (My God, if Olivetti had had a memory she would have written an autobiography!) However this memory could only remember my mistakes, and seemed to spend more time going backwards obliterating words than it did going forwards.

You didn't fit it with spools of ribbon winding sinuously through hoops and sprockets, you fed it with cartridges. Quite literally in the end, for it contrived to digest nearly a complete roll of film in its gut before expiring with a pitiful and extended peep. I realised how the times had changed when the man in the shop, instead of offering to mend the machine, tried to sell me something with winking lights and a purr, whose star feature apparently was that of 'self-justifying'.

Well, a typewriter that offers self-justification is either inordinately arrogant or hopelessly complex for me. It is yet another witness to the truth of McLuhan's assertion that the medium has become the message. Like hi-fi enthusiasts who are so absorbed in assessing the performance of their woofers and tweeters that they forget they are listening to music, so writers are being ruined by technology. The ultimate accolade soon will not be 'how interesting' but 'what a beautifully self-justified, proportionally-spaced piece of writing'.

I fear it is already irrelevant. When Mark Twain handed in the first 41 book manuscript in history to be typewritten, you can bet there was some publisher's reader who gave a wry smile, shook his head and declared that this trendy form of writing wouldn't last, mark his words. Of course he was quite right, it hasn't. There are offices already where the typewriter is extinct; offices once animated by the clatter of shift-keys and the ping of carriage returns, where now the silence of the morgue reigns and faces reflect the ghostly green of the VDUs like the living dead.

Where now are the litter-baskets brimming with crumpled foolscap? Where the fingers blackened with carbon paper? Where the heady scent of liquid Tippex, the delicate brushstrokes over rogue letters? Fading from the memory, before the remorseless advance of the word-processor. The very phrase is ominous. Words are to be wrestled with, teased out, agonised over – but never processed, like peas. But the canning process has already begun, when one machine can store whole chunks of text to be selected and reassembled to cover any eventuality, while on the other side of town another machine has stored all possible replies. They could correspond with one another *ad infinitum*.

No doubt I shall succumb in the end, and learn to stare at a blank screen for hours instead. And then if, through some digital malfunction, I succeed in wiping out a whole chapter at a stroke I can always get my little Olivetti out of retirement, and carry on typing.

PLASTIC FOR YOUR THOUGHTS

t hasn't gone yet, but it's going. The fuel of all economies, the *sine qua non* of wealth, the medium of exchange, is on the way out. This may not necessarily be any cause for alarm, but it is most certainly one of regret. I refer to cash.

Hard cash. Soft cash. Money, metal money. And paper too, paper money. Cash. The stuff you keep in your pockets and wallets and French peasants keep underneath their beds. We are seeing the last days

43

of it. It is being killed by clever plastic cards and cleverer computers. It cannot keep up with modern technology. It cannot keep up with inflation. Bad money drives out good, and plastic drives out cash.

Why bother? Plastic cards and computers are more convenient, many say. Are they? Cash transactions are far quicker and simpler than those involving plastic. It is as easy to carry cash around as a wallet full of plastic cards. Cash is real: nobody has to check your cash. There are no furtive telephone inquiries to see if your credit is sound when you are paying with cash. Plastic may be good for banks and good for shops and good for credit companies; but what is good for them is not necessarily good for your average customer, not necessarily any good at all. Customers have not created the demand for plastic. That demand has come from the suppliers, the banks and the credit companies, which nowadays practically force their plastic upon you. It must be good for them, or else they would not be so keen. What is good for them is not necessarily good for the rest of us.

There are sound enough economic reasons for regretting the disappearance of cash. Cash, to work, requires a stable value. There was a time when everybody knew perfectly well that cash needed to be genuine. Best, therefore, if it was made of real sterling silver. Real unadulterated gold. No tainted money, no money which could be watered down.

Once paper came into it, governments could start printing money. This was much easier than debasing the coinage. Inflation became a tool which governments found very easy to use. But even paper money poses problems for cheating governments. When great filthy wads of the stuff are necessary for the most modest purchases, it becomes evident to everyone that there is something very rotten in the state of the economy. When paper pound notes went out, we knew the government had debased the coinage all right.

But when cash disappears entirely, or almost entirely, and all exchange is done through plastic cards and clever computers we'll have no physical evidence in our pockets to remind us that we are ruled with irresponsible profligacy. There may still be the Retail Price Index, but it is not the same as the constant reminder of what is going on in your pockets and wallets, as they become heavier and heavier and fuller and fuller with increasingly worthless cash (and anyway, the RPI is such a nuisance nowadays to governments that soon enough it will be RIP for the RPI).

I well remember the shock when I was asked for my credit card or account number after I had bought some shirts and underpants at Garfinkel's in Washington back, I think, in 1968. "It's all right," I said, "I'll pay cash." It wasn't all right. They had got rid of cash. They had no means of taking it. It took half an hour to pay in cash. And I remember, too, holding out against credit cards in England, only to find that when I offered to pay by cheque, my cheques were suddenly treated as worthless, not being accompanied by any piece of plastic. Now, I am forever being offered new plastic cards, extra credit, easy money, money cheap by nature and easy, if dear, to borrow. The wonder is not that we have inflation, but that it is as low as it is. You beat inflation by increasing your debt and your increased debt cheapens money and increases inflation: that's the way the cookie crumbles. It's OK for heavy borrowers and lazy governments. No one really minds inflation except old people on fixed incomes, and who really cares about them?

Cash, now, that was different. When I was born pennies from my great-great-grandfather's time were still in use and still worth a penny, give or take a farthing or so. You could buy quite a lot with a penny in the Thirties. Even in the Forties and early Fifties, if you had some silver in your pocket you had enough for a drink and a meal. There was still some probity left in public finances. We used to have a three-course supper in the Fulham Road for two and ninepence. A child's eye widened at a half-a-crown, a pound note was a valuable thing, a fiver and you were wealthy. Remember those white fivers? Paper money was never so beautiful, never so good. Of course it was better in the really sound old days of gold sovereigns, when you could travel Europe for months in style, with a purse of sovereigns secure in a waistbelt, and no need of travellers' cheques or money-changers or even of passports, come to that. But still, money remained more or less as it was. Cash was cash, and held its value, and the first mortgage I took out was at four per cent. You could still buy things with the money in your pocket, even with the coppers. If your trouser pockets jangled when you put your hands in them you were not broke, you were not short of a bob or two, you could walk with a bit of confidence. Now, coppers are useless and the silver not much better. The weight of cash I carry around does not diminish; only its value, only its use.

Copper is rubbish; cupro-nickel is almost as useless. We might as well get rid of it. And paper money too. It is all becoming garbage. Let's throw it all away. Here's to life with plastic cards and computers! Here's to life on credit!

YOUR DINNER'S IN THE MORGUE

I expect everyone has their own memory of food – you know, that stuff we all used to eat and enjoy without a second thought.

It would probably surprise a lot of young people today to learn that there used to be a time when a healthy adult male could tuck into a suet pudding or a chicken liver pâté without the word 'cholesterol' once crossing his mind. Milk was good for you – and butter and cheese and cream kept you healthy! Ah! how things have changed.

47

Do you remember those halcyon days when it was possible to eat eggs? Yes, I know it must sound incredible to young people today, but people really did used to eat eggs. Not only did they eat them, but they never got ill or died as a result. In fact they used to eat eggs without even knowing the words enteritis B or salmonella. You youngsters may gape in amazement, but I tell you it's true. We ate eggs scrambled, soft-boiled, sunny-side-up . . . even raw eggs in a glass of whisky or else whipped up into a delightful creamy substance known as 'mayonnaise'. But nowadays the government warns us not to touch such things even when we can find them. A hard-boiled egg is all the servants of the state will allow us now and then, one suspects, only so that they can claim that there's nothing – absolutely nothing – wrong with the British egg industry.

Moreover, it was possible, in those days, to eat these eggs without that nagging question at the back of one's mind: 'Is this really a free-range egg – or did they just put that on the label to make us feel better?' In actual fact the regulations that control what can be put on the labels of egg boxes nowadays are quite specific: if the label says 'free-range' the eggs have to have been laid by hens kept at no greater density than 20 birds to a tennis court. If they are 'semi-intensive' – no more than 80 birds to a tennis court, 'deep-litter' means 1,300 to a tennis court, and 'perchery or barn eggs' on the label means no more than 5,000 birds to a tennis court – although good luck trying to count them! If they are 'battery eggs' you can nail the hens to the perch for all the regulations say.

Before the death of food as we know it, there was something else we were able to eat – do you remember it? It was red, it tasted really scrummy, and it was called 'beef'. There was definitely no problem with beef. It was the staple of Old England. We used to eat it rare or even raw in 'steak tartare', but now we shall be doing that no longer. Of course, they took the taste away long ago, when they started applying growth hormones to the animals and feeding them on grain all the time. But then

48

they went one better, someone had the bright idea of turning cows into carnivores, getting them to eat sheep's brains and – bingo – BSE had arrived! RIP steak tartare . . .

In those days, too, you could eat Welsh lamb without worrying whether it had come from Snowdonia – from one of the 420 Welsh farms that still have a ban on their meat because of the radioactive fall-out from Chernobyl. You could eat fish from the Irish Sea without worrying about radioactive contamination from Sellafield, garlic pâté without worrying about listeria and buns without worrying about tartrazine. Even flour wasn't matured by having chlorine pushed through it and the white bread didn't have BHT but did have taste.

Talking of taste, do you remember 'apples'? They were wonderful things with wonderful names: Russets, Worcesters, Bramleys Seedlings, Grenadiers, Sturmers, Blenheim Oranges and so on. Where have they gone? Many varieties were made illegal by the EC – illegal to sell the seeds or even give them away, as the mandarins of Brussels sought to iron out non-conformity. Most of the varieties died of despair: seeing the serried rows of Golden Delicious on the supermarket shelves, they knew there was no place for them in this pre-packaged age.

In the United States, of the 7,098 varieties of American apple that were common last century, 6,121 are now extinct. In Belgium, the 600 varieties that filled their orchards in years gone by have been reduced to five. And of the poor, tasteless, shiny, cardboard specimens that now survive in the neon-lit displays across the world, you daren't actually eat them for fear of what the alar with which they've been sprayed will do to you.

My golly! Before the death of food it was even possible to drink British water straight from the tap without your hair turning green from aluminium poisoning (as happened to the good people of Camelford) and without finding larvae (as Londoners did last year). British water is now no more – in this land surrounded by water; that

49

which hasn't been poisoned with pesticides or polluted with fertilisers has been bought up by the French.

How did food die? It was a slow, lingering death due to multiple causes. Some people suspect foul play, with agribusiness and the food industry high on the list of suspects. However, investigations have often been hampered by the government's policy of protecting the suspects at all costs.

Two years ago the government threatened scientists with prosecution under the Official Secrets Act if they revealed what they knew about the hormone drug BST (Bovine Somatotropin) which is used to increase milk yields in cattle. In the same year the Treasury blocked an enquiry into the salmonella business and in 1990 the Food Safety Bill threatened health inspectors with up to two years in prison if they disclosed new food dangers to the public.

So, as I write, the memory of food still abides and, maybe, there is still a last flicker of life. There are, after all, signs of hope. But should food pass the way of all flesh, grain and vegetable matter, it will be greatly missed by those who knew it. My abiding sadness, however, is that those who have been brought up on frozen fish fingers and Big Macs (please don't sue) and the processed products of the processed minds of this processed civilisation will never have the faintest idea of what they are missing – or even that they are missing anything at all.

DON'T RING US, JUST TRILL

· ·

· ·

One of those bells that now and then rings. Rang. Rung. All done. Only a few years ago the sound a telephone made was so important, so downright persuasive, if a primitive man were to have stumbled on one ringing in the middle of the jungle, he would probably have fallen on his knees in wonder; then, sensing its insistent message, he would have raised the receiver cautiously to his ear and heard a civilised voice asking for Doctor Livingstone. Now, however, the modern telephone has lost all resonance and authority, and I dare say he'd squash the damn thing under his big, calloused foot while it chirruped like an affronted cricket. Answer it? Needs must. But the temptation is to throw it out the window and see if it flies away. Or feed it to the goldfish.

How the heart used to leap at its plangent summons! I can remember even as a toddler, stumbling across the garden to get to it first for the mischievous pleasure of delivering long descriptions of what I was wearing to adults who were begging to be passed to my mother. And that, I want you to know, was merely an American telephone that went 'brunnnng-pause-brunnng', not even a British telephone that in a demonstration of rare national overstatement went 'brunnnng-brunnng-pause-brunnnng'. But those were the days when the ring of any telephone had irresistible power, not the gnat-like irritant it has become, and its reverberation inspired hope of adventure, foreign travel, money, love! Then, when it rang, one ran eagerly with open heart and mind to answer it. Now, one wants to swat the nasty brute.

And what a pretty thing the phone used to be. Do you recall? As perfect as a seashell, it could have struggled up through the aeons – a hit here, a miss there – to emerge finally as a natural triumph. Think of it! One simple design that stretched comfortably from every human ear to every human mouth so pop stars and others with unusually big heads could use precisely the same instrument as nuns and paupers. Remember how its waisted mid-section fitted almost sensually into any hand? A flow of wit and brilliance seemed to be invited by the two dear little trumpets upturned at either end, and words clamoured to be spoken into their tiny privacy. (World travellers may recollect that in France ordinary household telephones always had extra earpieces attached, presumably to facilitate communication within the ménage à trois.)

Ah me! Oh my! All done now. Alexander Graham Bell's great achievement diminished virtually overnight to something that vaguely resembles a boot stretcher. Gone the inviting and democratic shape of the old phone, to be replaced by a rough oblong which, I must say, is of blatantly sexist design. (Because the new telephones lack indentations, they must be held tight against the cheek during use. Surely, I'm not the only female who must periodically clean her receiver with make-up remover?)

Of course, absolutely the only colour a telephone was intended to be is black. Anything else is perverse, unnatural, and decadent. Black is solid, black is important, and often a telephone was the single black object a household contained: unique, as it deserved to be. Black sets the imagination dreaming and makes a suitable background on which to sprinkle words of vivid or delicate emotion. I mean, the very idea of talking to one's lover through lime green is evil; and as for contacting the bank manager on a red line, well it's hardly what one could call a comforting colour coding, is it? When it comes to shaping telephones into a semblance of other things, I shall not dignify the trend by mentioning it here. Except to say that those of you who like your words filtered through a miniature Mickey Mouse or a plastic replica of Venus de Milo, that's your business, I suppose. But please don't ring me. Ring each other.

'To ring', a noble infinitive which in this context, strictly speaking, should give way to lesser verbs more suited to the sound of modern telephones: 'to chirrup', as I've mentioned, 'to warble', 'to trill', even 'to squeak you up on Saturday'. But 'to ring' no more. Nor in truth and logic do we any longer dial. I used to adore dialling, sometimes with the rubber tip of a pencil. There was the cheery 'whizz' followed by that charming 'chukkachukkachukka . . .' long or short, depending upon the finger's location on the dial. (Policemen and FBI agents in the vicinity could reproduce any number from the 'chukkas' they overheard. Can you imagine how many major crimes must have gone unsolved since we lost the honest dial and changed over to those secretive buttons?)

Speaking as a mother who is trying against odds to raise her son with
a feeling for the diversity and precision of his native tongue, how can I,
in conscience, ask the boy to 'dial granny's number' when we both
know he's actually going to have to punch it?

So far, I'll grant, my nostalgia has been for the material attributes of
the old phone: its shape, its sound, its colour, its sweet, swirling,
law-abiding dial. Yet, there is a more subtle issue to examine; a more
profound loss on what we philosophers call the existential level. I speak
as a master of the medium, by the way, a woman who has spent much
of her life on the telephone sending out messages of hope and laughter
as well as requests for peace, love, and pastrami sandwiches. Over the
years, I have set many wires thrumming with countless home truths
and – I'll admit it – hundreds of lies.

So take it from me, to punch a number is not to dial it, to hold a
receiver light as an empty corn-husk is not to feel the weight of serious
communication, and to wander about with a cordless instrument dusting
bookshelves or stirring the soup or even (can you believe?) scrabbling for
the soap at the bottom of the bath, while another human being pours his
very soul into one's ear, is not polite.

"Why do you sound so muffled?" I interrupted my own brilliant (if
I do say so myself) monologue on the nature of sexual attraction to
ask a friend the other day. "Sorry," he said, "I'm in the garden shed
looking for the insect spray." Alas and farewell, dead ringer! Thou wert.
But art not now. Thy nightingale's song gives way to flea-buzz. Thou
hast been well and truly bugged.

3

Dying Breeds

CONDUCTORS UNBECOMING

Not many days ago, the obituary appeared in the *Independent* of Douglas Scott. Mr Scott was the designer of London Transport's Routemaster bus. In a bold break with obituarial tradition, the appreciation featured a photograph not of the man, but of the bus. The back end of the bus.

Mr Scott was by all accounts a modest man. Somewhere up there in the eternal bus-garage, he would have chuckled with pleasure at this, the greatest possible compliment to his wonderful design. But my own 'In Memoriam' is not for Mr Scott, nor even for his incomparable bus. My lament is for neither an individual nor a motor vehicle, but for a concept which Mr Scott's Routemaster served with such splendid distinction: the concept of the conducted London omnibus. It is not dead yet, but it is in mortal danger. London Regional Transport has been trying to kill the conducted bus for decades. It brought in the ghastly opos (one person-operated buses, where the driver takes the fares) with unimaginable hoo-hah, and the public was not impressed. It brought in more, with new designs, and still the public was not impressed. It phased out the Routemaster, with its conductor, on route after route, and with each conductor's demise, public resentment grew. Now, 30 years on, just a few Routemasters remain on the routes even LRT dares not pretend can run without a conductor.

We are prone, in public transport, to nostalgia. The horse, the tram, the electric bus – each in its time has given way to something better, but never without fulsome lamentation. We are used to sentimentality, and discount it.

But the demise of the conducted bus arouses not sentimental regret – after it has gone – but practical fury, while it is still with us, dying. Here is a concept which works, under threat from a concept which doesn't. Never in the history of public transport in our metropolis has a change been pushed through against such long and consistent and sustained evidence that the public hates it, the operators hate it, the police hate it, and it doesn't work. If we had started with conductorless buses, I swear some bright spark in a university would have invented the concept of conductors, and we should all have leapt at the improvements they bring.

There may be among you readers who like my late friend, Ian Gow MP, affect not to know about buses. A colleague once persuaded Ian – bound for Westminster and with not a taxi in sight – to try the Number

11 bus from Victoria to the House of Commons. To much humorous protest the conductress got him sat down (he asked whether it would be cold outside, on top) whereupon he tried to tip her, while explaining that he was to be driven through the Commons Carriage Gates and dropped at the Members' Entrance.

She declined to make this diversion and refused the tip. I hope she realised Ian was joking.

He knew the score. For any who don't, let me remind you. The Routemaster conducted bus permits passengers: to climb in fast, through a wide space at the back, and sit down immediately, so that the driver can move straight off; to pay the conductor in their own time, and wait for change; to chat to the conductor about directions, or alternative buses; to enquire as to the opening hours of the Tower of London; to hop on or off at traffic lights, in traffic jams, or even when the bus is moving; to travel in central London at walking pace. Opo buses are slower.

The Routemaster permits the operator: to keep his vehicle moving, not stuck at bus-stops while the poor driver sells tickets to a great queue of would-be passengers, while half London's traffic piles up behind; to keep order in the bus (how can a driver deal with a yob who is being sick on the top deck in the back seat?); to keep track of who has paid what, and when they get off. The first law of bus travel is that almost everybody tries to cheat a bit, at all times.

The opo buses fail every one of these tests. In addition they rattle, break down constantly, and their windows mist up. They look like biscuit tins. They are rightly an object of loathing to passengers, staff and every other road user. They are slowly killing the habit of bus travel in our capital.

Can anything at all be said in their favour? Obviously the operator saves the conductor's measly wage. But at what cost in efficiency, morale and lost goodwill? Let LT try putting a twopenny surcharge onto tickets on conducted buses to test the market. I know which the passenger would

choose.

The biscuit tins are, finally, said to be safer. This is because passengers are trapped in them – or outside – until the driver has a spare moment to open the doors and judges this suitable. Thus is lost one of the last great urban thrills now left to the Londoner; the dice with death as you sprint alongside an accelerating Number 11 bus with a briefcase in your left hand and your right extended to catch the upright pole at precisely the right instant – and it has to be precise, when you make that leap.

Sometimes the passengers cheer. I have seen grown men weep with pride and relief. For children it is part of the process of growing up, when the weak are separated from the strong and prowess is rewarded with survival.

Routes 3, 9, 11, 12, 15 . . . the roll-call of honour! You few are the last of a kind. London Transport is out to get you! Hang on in there, and hold very tight, please. Ting, ting.

LODGING A BELATED PROTEST

I suppose they still exist somewhere but surely not in the mode that I remember. Indeed you never hear people even speak of lodgings anymore – far too bald and unvarnished a term for nowadays. If they were to get a mention they would probably be called, say, a transient domiciliary environment, presided over by a landperson or something equally neuter. Proper lodgings, anyway, require not only the

60

utilitarian terminology of ancient times like the 1950s but the furnishings, fashions and, most importantly, the attitudes of mind of the era.

Real lodgers, for example, would have their hair shorn high above their ears and at the back of the neck, well north of the collar of a 50 shilling suit, usually with a shiny seat. This was not entirely due to poverty, although that was usually present, more to the amount of polish that was applied to all visible surfaces. Lodgings were invariably old, chilly and decorated in the style of a police barracks but they were swept and scoured and buffed as if to remove all traces of a fatal epidemic. This ferocious level of cleanliness was tied in with the moral code of such establishments which, although fractured with great regularity on the quiet, was adhered to rigidly in public.

I encountered lodgings when I first came to London, my belongings wrapped in a spotted kerchief carried over my shoulder on the end of a stick. It was fully understood in those days that a man, a bachelor especially, would decline very quickly without a daily cooked breakfast and a substantial meal in the evening prepared and proffered by somebody else. Of the female gender of course.

It's puzzling now, though it wasn't at the time when I knew no better either. I had just left the Army where you had to learn to sew, iron, burnish, dust, sweep, make beds and leave the ablutions in far better condition than you would ever expect to find them. The Army was meant to make a man of you but turned you out much better equipped to get a job as a chambermaid.

You had discovered, though, that it was possible to live entirely on corned beef for astonishing periods, rather as a camel copes on a drink of water, and to sleep soundly anywhere that there was room to tilt your head. Above all you learned self-reliance which meant, in this context, that you didn't look to anybody else for any sort of assistance or sustenance unless you'd just been shot.

Why then was it not possible on returning to civilian life to fix up a satchel of iron rations and doss down in the park while finding one's feet? I don't know, but it wasn't. Nobody allowed it. A mother who had mopped her eyes, but squared her shoulders, as a troopship set sail carrying her son to certain death fighting the Fuzzy Wuzzys, or similar, became hysterical at the thought of the same lad settling in London in anything but much the same circumstances as he had enjoyed at home, aged six.

To meet this need there emerged a type of environment and a race of women who would act *in loco parentis* or, in my experience, in loco almost anything else, from wardress through to mistress. What a breed they were! In nearly every case cruel fate had forced them into a course of action as desperate as taking in lodgers, as the gruesome phrase of the period described their plight. If they had been blokes they would have joined the Foreign Legion.

My first landlady was Mrs Graunch, not her real name of course which was much more forbidding, as was the lady herself with her needle nose and eyes set like angry currants closely on either side of the bridge. If she had joined the Legion they would have made her up to sergeant immediately, without the five year probationary period.

Mean as muck, her parsimony extended from food through the electricity and water supplies even unto the toilet paper. Needing the type of control of her domain now exercised only by certain South American dictators, she would allow no imports in any of these categories and was ruthless in her hunt for contraband. In my room, the only privacy was a single small drawer with a key to it but that didn't keep her out. She would pick the lock, with her nose I think, in search of rolls, either cheese or toilet.

Eating was always a crucial component of life in lodgings. What distinguished them, if anything did, was the status of the lodger as an auxiliary, or supernumerary, member of a proper household, rather than some fly-by-night using an assumed name. It was important that a lodger should be seen with his feet beneath the table as firmly as once they might have been anchored in the stocks.

This led to some dramas, I can tell you. In my next place the landlady had been widowed formally, unlike Mrs Graunch who, I believe, had done her husband in. Here the man had merely caught a bus, but in the small of the back unfortunately, leaving debts and a child to be raised, a familiar set of circumstances in the lodging business. I've noticed that an unusual number of landladies' daughters have been spurred on by hardship to become singers, actresses, ballerinas and the like. The only chance in showbusiness for this daughter lay in her powerful resemblance to Arthur Scargill. Taken together with a vicious temper it was no wonder that her mother wished to marry her off, not least to leave her room free for another lodger. "Where are we off to tonight then, Mr Sandiman?" I can still hear her croon over the cornflakes. "Town Hall dance I think, Mrs Booby." (Honorifics flew back and forth in lodgings like the ball in a ping-pong match.) Mrs Booby would roll her eyes towards her daughter and produce a stream of vowels like those bubbles you can blow via a magical compound and a little hoop: "Oooooo, the Town Hall dance, Shirl!" she would carol as if Shirl and I had been planning the outing for weeks, but Shirl would merely growl and roll her lips back from her teeth like an angry cheetah.

As it happens a cheerful young salesman joined us, a single lodger being as rare as an only child in those days, and he took to her so quickly that he pressed my foot by mistake under the table on the very first evening. When Shirl produced a brilliant smile and took off her horn-rims, I knew it was time to move on and fetched up in a house where the landlady had no less than six husbands while I was there, but all of them other people's, and nibbled at her lodgers in between times as if they were snacks.

Lodgings became an endangered and then an extinct species as this type of warm interaction fell foul of a century now hell-bent on high

63

technology and solitary supremacy. Launderettes took care of the washing and made life possible with a single pair of sheets. The terror of starvation faded in the face of the fast food joints but so, of course, did the great eating rituals. Mums stopped worrying except about whether they could get back to work on the same day as giving birth. The scene was set for the bed-sitter, the flat, even the house. I have two now but rarely as much fun as I did in those of Mrs Graunch, Mrs Booby and the rest.

THE SETTING OF THE STARS

To celebrate Hollywood's centenary as the West's leading manufacturer and repository of the twin gods Fame and Fortune, an international poll was held. Who were the film capital's greatest ever stars? A simple question which, like all the simplest questions, would seem open to endless debate or downright unanswerable.

Not so. Back came the overwhelming replies. Katharine Hepburn

romped home for the ladies with the equally durable Bette Davis
warmly on her heels. Clark Gable and Cary Grant mopped up on behalf
of the men. The rest – the Redfords and the Dunaways, the Streeps
and the Streisands, the Hoffmans and the Newmans, the Cruises and the
Kellys – all were ranked as also-rans. All of which proved what I have long
suspected and recently regretted. Today there are no stars.

Oh, there are fine and distinguished actors, charismatic creatures, too,
who are adored or lusted after; and there are those who go on being
famous merely for being famous, as the saying goes. But none of them
fulfils that old-fashioned Hollywood definition of a star. Distant,
unattainable and externally shining forth with a magical quality all of its
own. Today we have only a collection of erratic meteorites masquerading
as stars because daily, in the media, their names are hyped as such with
the prefix 'super' or 'mega' attached for hard-sell. Yet, as that great
amorphic mass, the being known as Joe Public, has just determined, real
stars are a vanished or vanishing configuration.

The indestructible Bette Davis herself once tried to explain the
inexplicable quality which puts these people above their peers, even
when they are shown in private to be as flawed and fallible as any other
mortal.

"A star is someone who, when his or her name goes up above a
marquee, causes a queue to form below it," reported Miss Davis in her
own cryptic style. And for many years that is what I truly believed to be
so, passing on this received wisdom in lectures, articles and countless dinner
conversations. Imagine my shock to see Miss Davis's maxim confounded
recently when long lines of fan-fodder lined up beneath the marquee
of a London theatre where a cast of decent jobbing actors from the
television series 'Allo, Allo' were giving what I fervently trust to be a
lot less than their all in a dismally mounted stage version of that show.

Had I been introduced to most of this motley at a party previously,
I might easily have enquired in all innocence what they did for a living. By

today's devalued and departing standards, however, they clearly pass for stars. Television and the tabloids have conferred the status; but in name only. Legends are made by a different chemistry entirely.

Of course the devaluing process set in with the television era. Andy Warhol grasped and exploited its cheap potential early on when he rightly claimed: "Soon everyone will be famous for 15 minutes." A prospect which we children of the late Fifties and early Sixties deemed full of excitement and challenge. And lo, it came to pass. More and more of us found ourselves knowing or on nodding acquaintance with more and more people whose names flashed briefly into the national consciousness. Some of us even made it to the foothills of fame ourselves, by appearing on panel games and discussion programmes where instant pundits are a dime a dozen.

But this was not stardom as we all once knew it, staring up entranced at giant images on the silver screen or gazing agog and awestruck to see a legend materialise behind the footlights of some red plush theatre. No. Today the term household name is roughly synonymous with Harpic or Kellogg's cornflakes; one more instantly recognisable commodity daily flogged on and by the flickering box in the corner of our own humdrum home.

When television first arrived, like the rest of my generation I watched its earliest personalities with something of the fervour I reserved for Gable or Garland on the big screen, or Olivier and Evans on the stage. Yet without knowing it, we were subscribing to the Marshall McLuhan thesis that 'the medium is the message'. The miracle was television itself, not the men and women it made familiar. For we all know what familiarity breeds, don't we?

Well, eventually I did appear on panels with the likes of the enduring Miss Barbara Kelly and the delightful Miss Katie Boyle, two of the survivors from those long-ago original pioneering days. But by then I had the measure of television's ability to diminish one's professional standing

67

in the eyes of the public rather than enhance it. As a critic of a national daily paper, I had enjoyed a modest, if treasured and highly over-rated, reputation as a member of that exclusive club whose pronouncements cast chills down the spines of powerful producers and feted performers alike.

Now I found myself being inexplicably greeted in the street by strangers – and with such astonishing familiarity I was sure I must be suffering from some Kafka-esque lapse of memory. "Blimey, Jackie! You've shrunk since Sunday!" called out a burly builder enigmatically, clambering down some scaffolding in Covent Garden to slap me heartily on the back. In my winded state it took some time to work out that on Sunday I'd featured in a game of 'Tell The Truth', recorded some nine months before. What price quarter of an hour's fame? And what size his screen? So if such a minor player in the second league of the fame game can sink in the mud, how can such faltering legends as Elizabeth Taylor surrender their omnipotent status on the slippery slopes of the TV soaps?

The greatest, most luminous stars instinctively fought shy of such an earth-bound medium when television first arrived. And their instinct was true. Television is the natural enemy of mystique, the star's only real defence of his or her stock-in-trade. The octogenarian Marlene Dietrich, for example, chooses these days to cloister herself in the seclusion of her Paris flat rather than allow the camera of some passing paparazzo to destroy the myth of her fabled beauty – echoing exactly the declining days of the screen's first real goddess, Mary Pickford.

Some may see this as the vanity of old women; I see it as the jealous protection of a lifelong investment – their own legend – and a realistic acknowledgment of their unreal status. Not for them the casual overfamiliarities of a brash public tutored to treat its newer idols as nothing rarer than the flowerpot on top of the telly or the plates on the kitchen dresser. Theirs was the scarcity value of their own uniqueness.

One-off creatures sustained by the old studio system on screen, or by the glamour and sense of occasion a theatre itself imparted.

Once I had dinner with Dame Edith Evans, one of the last great autocrats of the British stage. All conversation in the little restaurant where we dined dropped to hushed reverence the moment she appeared at the door, except of course for Dame Edith's which quavered eccentrically over a hundred and one topics on which she pronounced for all to hear. Eventually a fellow diner plucked up the courage to interrupt her flow and ask for her autograph. The Dame inspected his proffered piece of paper as if for cleanliness or hidden messages and then, in uncharacteristic silence, signed her name. The man had not time to murmur his thanks before she announced to no one in particular, "I have never understood why people want autographs. I never did!"

What a rude awakening would have awaited her had she chosen to end her days appearing on the small screen as a regular supplement to the wallpaper in every living room in the land. The hurly-burly of commonplace chit-chat was quite foreign to her style and her stature as a star. Even the great and glorious Maggie Smith, once seen on television, becomes reduced to a cipher of the individual role that found favour with the viewer, just as 'Coronation Street's lamented Pat Phoenix became 'Elsie' to all who had hailed her. Visiting Miss Smith in her remote Sussex farmhouse, I asked what effect her presence had had in the sleepy rural community.

"Oh, nil," she assured me! "If I walk the dog down the lane they might shout things like 'Lovely day Miss Brophy!'" Only this superior actress's innate vulnerability and natural classiness prevent her retorting "Brodie's the name," I suspect. But can you imagine Katharine Hepburn ever being hailed as the African Queen?

BYE, BYE BLACK SHEEP

"The man is an absolute cad." The speaker was an ambassador; not a British diplomat sent to lie abroad for his country, but a foreign one at the Court of St James's. He had learned his English well, but some 50 years ago, and the idiom he used was preserved in the clear amber of time; no Englishman nowadays would use the word cad. It is one of the most interesting words in the language, but it has only had a life of about 100 years. In that time it subtly changed its meaning, and then expired for want of use. It is a grievous business, for the word had a sleazy charm, and the chap it described had a colourful role in our nation's annals. Life was never dull when there were cads around.

The golden – or perhaps we should say the chromium – age of the cad was the 1930s: epoch of the cocktail-shaker, brothel-creeper and silver cigarette case. He has customarily left his school, university or regiment under some sort of cloud. He is essentially an Englishman. A Welsh cad is a tautology, a Scottish cad an improbability, and an Irish cad frankly an absurdity. His rank is invariably captain. Subalterns are too green to be cads; majors too grey.

Captain Grimes, the sublime bounder in Evelyn Waugh's great novel 'Decline and Fall', remains the doyen of his calling, though the most thorough-going rotter in 20th century English fiction is surely Captain Edward Fox-Ingleby, hero of A. G. MacDonnell's delicious satire on the English upper class, 'Autobiography of a Cad'. Edward's particular hero was E. E. Smith, later Lord Birkenhead; and it is interesting to remember that Clementine Churchill endured much from Winston's three bosom friends, none of whom had any pretensions to be gentlemen, and whom she immortalised as the three terrible Bs – Birkenhead, Bracken and Beaverbrook.

Yet Winston himself of course was thought distinctly unsound for much of his career. When Clementine was first introduced to him at a ball, her partner asked her why she had been talking to 'that frightful fellow'. When the frightful fellow became war premier in 1940, however, he called on the two terrible Bs still around, Beaverbrook and Bracken, to be part of his inner councils. So cads can have their uses, especially when you are up against a bounder like Hitler.

Indeed, the cad usually turns out to be a good man in a tight corner. Capel Maturin, for instance, in Michael Arlen's 'The Ace of Cads', has won the DAO and Bar. He has been cashiered from the Brigade of Guards for 71 what must nowadays seem a relatively minor offence: pouring wine in a restaurant over a conductor who persisted in playing Mendelssohn's *Spring Song* after being asked three times to desist. It's fascinating to see what a sinister and persuasive role Mendelssohn plays in the life of cads. In the famous hotel scene from 'The Great Gatsby', when the good-for-nothing Tom Buchanan picks a quarrel with Gatsby, the portentous chords of Mendelssohn's *Wedding March* float up from the ballroom below. Harry Faversham, branded a coward in 'The Four Feathers', has Mendelssohn's *Melusine* overture played to him insistently on the violin by Ethne, surely the most ineffably awful girl in the whole panoply of English literature. Harry's reaction is the only possible one – to go off and suffer unspeakable privations in the desert for six years to redeem the white feather she has so callously given him.

All the cads we have examined so far are gentlemen who have given up their code. They know how to behave, but fail to do so. When the Western Brothers, those modish comedians of yesteryear, exhorted their audiences to 'play the game, you cads,' they implicitly accepted that cads knew the rules, but broke them. Nevertheless, certain residual tribal loyalties were still called on. ('Don't do the dirty on an Old Narkovian; try to be a decent sort of swine.') The sentiment was echoed by that prince among cads, George Sanders. As he remarked in his autobiography, 'Memoirs of a Professional Cad': 'I was beastly but I was never coarse. I was a high-class sort of heel.'

The cad came a long way in his 100 years. He started in 1831 as a contemptuous term used by Oxford undergraduates for townsmen, and within ten years was any vulgar or ill-bred fellow. In Compton Mackenzie's celebrated Oxford novel 'Sinister Street', the hero, Michael Fane, and some of his friends decide to rag the rooms of a fellow undergraduate called Smithers. What has Smithers done? Nothing, but he is a cad; a poor scholar, a carpenter's son with a cockney accent, and he is to be ragged for his general bearing and plebeian origin. The irony is that insofar as the word still means anything in England, it is Fane and his friends who are now cads, not Smithers.

The cad's weaknesses are girls, gin and gee-gees, usually in that order. The trouble is that women are fond of them, and they know it. In that immortal exchange in 'My Fair Lady', Colonel Pickering gallantly tries to make sure Henry Higgins is a fit person to tutor Eliza Doolittle. "Are you," he inquires, "a man of good character where women are concerned?" Higgins has the only possible answer: "Have you ever met a man of good character where women are concerned?" Precisely; we are all cads nowadays.

GENTLEMEN AND PLAYERS

I t was, as if it could have been anyone else, the late Arthur Marshall who was mourning in this column a couple of years ago the disappearance of the drawing-room comedy and with it the grande dame of ample proportions. Sadly we have now also lost her male counterpart, the gentleman actor: the passing this year of Wilfrid Hyde White and last year of Sir Rex Harrison marked the end of a theatrical line that went back to Gerald du Maurier and Charles Hawtrey at the very beginning of this century, the first men to light cigarettes on a stage and to be seen in the very same three-piece suits which they had been wearing for lunch at the Garrick.

The curious thing about the gentleman actor was the speed of his arrival on stage: until the knighthood of Henry Irving in 1895, actors had all been considered rogues and/or vagabonds, unacceptable in polite society and certainly not the kind of chaps to be allowed anywhere near a decent man's daughter or, heaven forfend, his son.

But men like Hawtrey and du Maurier were the first to realise that if, in the wake of Irving, the actor was ever to achieve social respectability, then they had to be seen to be gentlemen on stage and off. Noel Coward was taught his comic trade by Charles Hawtrey (not to be confused with a late actor of the same name who turned up in countless 'Carry Ons'), whose timing was at its immaculate best when removing a cigarette from its case downstage left and placing it in a holder before crossing upstage right. My father Robert remembers being much influenced in the 1920s by a long-forgotten actor called Basil Loder, whose role was always that of the leading actor's Best Friend: he would appear early in act one to announce that he was "just tootling off to the golf course", and then reappear to share a cocktail in act two before the denouement in act three. It was a pleasant, harmless kind of existence and the great attraction was that the people who conveyed it on stage seemed also to be able to afford it in real life: a little light golf in the morning, a little light acting at the matinée.

Gentleman-acting was to some extent the art of the minimal: two of its best exponents, the film star David Niven and the playwright/actor Hugh Williams, once found themselves supporting a rather more histrionic actor, Laurence Olivier, in 'Wuthering Heights': "What do you plan to do in this scene, old boy?" Williams asked Niven on the set. "I didn't think I'd do very much here," replied Niven. "No, no," said Williams in some alarm, "I'm doing nothing in this scene."

It also depended greatly on familiarity and reassurance: "Ah," said Rex Harrison once, greeting my father whom he had scarcely met since drama school and the 1939 film of 'Major Barbara', but whom he had just seen on television in 'This Is Your Life', "I would never dare to do a programme like that, not with all my ex-wives and the suicides and all that. But then Robert, since we left drama school, your life has been so very different to mine. I mean, in your case one wife, one family, one home, and, if I may say so, one performance."

In fact of course it was Rex who never changed a raised eyebrow, let alone a performance: Guinness and Olivier were welcome to hide away behind false noses or elaborate hairpieces or funny walks, but for the gentleman actor the art was to be instantly recognisable, and therefore reassuring to audiences who expected of them rather what they expected of master chefs or great hoteliers: an evening of undemanding, escapist pleasure.

The gentleman actor would occasionally venture into Shaw but never into Shakespeare; Rattigan and Lonsdale certainly, Pinero but never Pinter, Anouilh sometimes, but never Racine. The art was above all one of superlative comic timing, something that nearly all of them carried through into their private, off-stage lives. Somebody in California once asked Wilfrid Hyde White, then close to ninety, why he had left England so abruptly. "Two reasons, my dear fellah," said Wilfie, "couldn't bear my second wife, couldn't bear the Inland Revenue." And then, with an exquisitely timed pause, he added: "That was a very caddish thing I just said, about the Inland Revenue." On another occasion, up before a judge in the bankruptcy courts, Hyde White declined to pass on any of his racing tips: "Ho, ho, Your Honour, wouldn't do at all. Not unless you'd like us to change places?"

But by the time he settled in California, the curtain had really come down on the gentleman actor: one or two of a slightly younger generation, David Tomlinson and Ian Carmichael, kept the tradition going for a while but as the scripts dried up, so too did the convention of snobbery-with-violence, that combination of elegant tailoring and lethal wit. For actors like Harrison, what mattered more than any cuts in the script was the cut of his suit, and that is not a tradition which can be explained to any modern actor in jeans and a sweatshirt. Gentleman actors had their plays tailor-made: Lonsdale would write du Maurier's last acts once they had gone into rehearsal and worked out together what kind of play it was going to be, just as Ben Travers would fix his farces for Tom Walls and Ralph Lynn once he had discovered what they wanted to do next.

No dramatist today expects to work in the fashion of a short-order cook, and it is therefore they and the director who are in the ascendant, with scripts regarded as complete before rehearsals begin. In the day of the gentleman actor, the dramatist and the director were essentially part of the stage crew, at the beck and call of the actor: "Do sit down," Harrison is reputed to have bellowed at one of his directors, "and I'll find you something to do in a minute." "Damn useful little chap," said Hyde White of one of his playwrights, "always takes my coat in the morning and hands it back at the end of rehearsal."

Not exactly the treatment accorded today to Sir Peter Hall or Tom Stoppard, which may be why the gentleman actor has gone the way of the three-act play and the interval tea and biscuits on a tray. Luckily a little of their craft is still preserved on film: next time television gives you the chance, have another look at Harrison and Hyde White in their only ever meeting, for the 'Rain in Spain' sequence of 'My Fair Lady'. It was the last dance of the gentleman actor.

On my way to the office the other morning, I stopped off to buy a potato peeler. Nothing complicated, not one of those gadgets that can string beans at one end and wash windows at the other, just a straightforward peeler.

"Excuse me," I asked the young man kneeling in front of a stack of jelly moulds in the basement, "where are the potato peelers?" "I haven't the faintest idea," he replied. "Oh I'm so sorry," I blurted, "I thought you worked here." "I do," he said, "but I'm on loan from bedding. They're short-staffed this week. I think I saw tin-openers the other side of that pillar, though, so they could be somewhere round there being the same sort of thing."

I thanked the young man who I noticed had a slightly gloomy air about him, due, no doubt, to years of trying to peel potatoes with a tin-opener and approached the far side of the pillar. A bank of ironing boards standing bolt upright, like a platoon of soldiers, confronted me, to the right shelves full of non-stick saucepans stretched into the distance, to the left salad bowls rose like minarets, not a potato peeler or a tin-opener in sight. And then just as I was thinking I'd leave it for another day a woman in a blue overall pushing a trolley full of mops and brooms rounded the corner.

"Excuse me," I said, "do you happen to know where the potato peelers are?" "I'm not officially on the floor," replied the mop woman mysteriously. "I'm stocktaking, but last time I saw them they were three aisles along, in electrical." "I don't want an electric peeler," I said, "just an ordinary hand-held job with a wooden handle. Isn't there anyone to ask?"

The mop woman looked at her watch. "Let me see. Mrs Wilmott is still on coffee break and I know Miss Sharpley is dealing with a customer return. If you wait here I'll see if I can find Mrs Braithwaite. I think she's in small household." While I waited for Mrs Braithwaite, several hopeless customers with the air of lost souls newly arrived in the Underworld asked me to direct them to thermos flasks, plugs and hoover bags.

"Where are the ironing boards?" a woman with three weeping children and a hysterical note in her own voice asked. Here was one I did know. "They're over on the right behind bakeware," I said. "Thank heavens I've at last found someone who can help," she said. "What size replacement cover do I need for the Lady Jane Executive model, with   79 adjustable sleeve stand?" I said I didn't actually work in the shop but had happened to notice ironing boards in my search for a potato peeler. "Well you needn't waste your time," said the woman with the three weeping children, "they've run out of potato peelers unless you want an electric one which can also string beans."

Sometimes you can just glimpse the back of one at the other end of a long aisle, but by the time you've raced to the spot she has disappeared. Sometimes you feel the only way to attract someone's attention would be to light a small bonfire, but even then the chances are they'd all be on coffee break. Quite by chance the other day, looking for someone to advise me on socks, I came upon what was clearly a cunningly camouflaged hide-out, in the lee of a display unit full of thick ribbed tights, half-hidden by the side of the escalator. Two assistants were sitting on a pile of cardboard boxes deep in conversation.

"So I said to him, if you feel like that you can keep your two weeks in Lloret and I'll make my own arrangements," the small thin one was saying. "Quite right too; oooh the nerve of it. Mind you that's men all over," said the big fat one. "Excuse me please," I began. "Course I wouldn't have minded if only he'd been frank with me from the start," continued the small thin one, popping a toffee into her mouth, "but to suddenly spring it on me like that at the last minute." "Sneaky devils, men. Never trust a man further than you can throw him, I always say," agreed the big fat one who looked as though she'd thrown a few in her time.

"I quite agree, ladies," I interrupted boldly, "but in the meantime, could I trouble one of you to help me find a pair of pure cotton tennis socks to fit a size three shoe." The two assistants looked at me with loathing. The fat one rose heavily to her feet, stony faced. "It's all right, Lorraine," she said with the resignation of someone about to perform a nasty chore like unblocking a drain. "I'll deal with this."

Shop assistants in the old days didn't just know where everything was

– none of this 'if it's not out we haven't got it' nonsense – they were also prepared to give you advice on your purchase. I remember accompanying my Aunt Vera to Marshall and Snelgrove's many years ago to buy a hat. The assistant in Millinery was attentiveness personified. No drawer was left unopened, no tissue wrapping undisturbed in her quest for the perfect hat. Halfway through an assistant from Belts came to ask if they had any large carrier bags because Belts had run out and Scarves were at lunch. "You'll have to wait until I've finished serving Modom," snapped our assistant and then turning to my aunt she confided: "Sometimes it's just a war of nerves." The quest continued. Some 20 creations were now lined up in front of Aunt Vera. "I would say that with Modom's colouring she should perhaps go for the softer pastel shades," advised our assistant. "Apricot is always becoming to the more mature complexion." My aunt eventually whittled the selection down to two finalists, a straw boater and a linen cloche. "This is curious," said my aunt looking at both price tags. "How is it that this one smothered with roses is 25 guineas while the other one which has only two rather small flowers on it costs 35 guineas?"

"Modom is paying for the restraint," replied the assistant.

They always wore grey flannel bags — shapeless, voluminous, billowing trousers with maybe a gaudy striped tie to hold them up instead of a belt — but then the tracksuit was invented and our sporting life changed for ever.

There are those who think that the 'amateur' was obliterated when the MCC abolished the distinction between 'gentlemen' and 'players'. Hitherto the amateurs had stayed in different hotels, dressed in different changing rooms, approached the field of play through different gates, and worn different caps – known sardonically to the professionals as 'fancy hats'. In 1963 that all changed. From that moment in cricket everyone was equal and everyone the same. It's a key date. All the same I think it was the advent of the tracksuit and the demise of grey flannel bags which really killed off the amateur. The real amateur had to look determinedly casual. (Not for nothing was that famous amateur soccer team called 'The Corinthian Casuals'.) You can't look casual in a tracksuit any more than in shoes with 'Adidas' or 'Nike' written all over them or even shirts endorsed by Fred Perry.

The clothing is the outward and visible sign of the casual inner man. The old amateurs cultivated a highly developed style of languid nonchalance. They might have cared as much as John McEnroe but they were damned if they'd let it show. Thus C. B. Fry, the archetypal grey flannel bag man, was asked why, as holder of the world long jump record, he was not competing in the Athens Olympics. "My dear fellow," he replied, "I'd no idea they were on." And like CB they had a fearful tendency to be multi-talented. That other great cricketer W.G. Grace, for instance, scored his first century against Surrey at the Oval – 224 not out – and then the next day, while the match was still in progress, skived off to Crystal Palace and won the 440-yard hurdles in one minute ten seconds. Just for a lark.

There are no WGs or CBs any more, not least because initials are out of fashion. In the old days the pros had their initials after their names as in Hutton L. while the fancy hat amateurs had theirs in front as in P.B.H. May. Never anything as vulgar as a Christian name for a true blue amateur. The change in the church hasn't helped either. There was a time when all self-respecting cricket teams had at least one vicar. My mother's Somerset village of Martock, for example, boasted one called Prebendary Wickham. Wickham had played for Norfolk and was also the uncle of another old Somerset amateur, the writer R. C. 'Crusoe'

Robertson-Glasgow. (Amateurs tended to have funnier names than professionals.) Wickham kept wicket for Somerset. Here is a newspaper report of his appearance at Lord's: 'A peculiar picture presented itself at Lord's in the person of the Rev A. P. Wickham, the Somerset wicket-keeper, standing with his legs so far apart that his head just appeared above the wicket. He looked a queer figure even without his eccentric attire. He wore white leg guards with black knee pieces. Above these were grey trousers and a black band or sash. A white shirt and a brilliant parti-coloured harlequin cap completed his curious "get-up".'

They don't make cricketers, or vicars, like that any more. The last reverend cricketer of real distinction was Rev D. S. Sheppard, now the rather radical Bishop of Liverpool but once more famous as England's opening batsman and captain.

Schoolmasters were another great source of fancy hats. Micky Walford who captained the 1948 Olympic hockey team used to score centuries for Somerset in the summer holidays when he had finished teaching at Sherborne. So did D. R. W. Silk, now Warden of Radley. Guy Willatt managed to teach at Repton in the winter and captain Derbyshire in the summer. It couldn't happen now, not least for the very laudable reason that if some schoolmaster waltzed into a team in August he'd be doing a professional out of work.

Cricket was always the most obvious repository of cavalier, Corinthian amateurs but there have been prodigious examples in other sports. Rugby football is still an avowedly amateur game through and through, though it looks pretty 'shamateur' and tracksuited to me, with the possible exception of the great Andrew Ripley, still going strong for Rosslyn Park in his late thirties when he can get away from the bank. My favourite old-fashioned rugby amateur was A. J. F. 'Tony' O'Reilly.

84   As a very young man O'Reilly was an exciting and even glamorous

wing three-quarter, but he also embarked on a meteoric business career. By his mid-thirties he was managing director of Heinz in London. Suddenly Ireland, going through a bad patch, decided it was time to recall the old hero. Mr O'Reilly arrived by chauffeur-driven limousine at Twickenham for the game against England. He had become prone to the business lunch and was at least two stone overweight, and when Willy John McBride, the huge Ulster forward, saw him before the match he said mournfully, "Jesus, you're huge . . . your best attacking move today is to shake your jowls at your opposite number." O'Reilly had an intentionally subdued game but he had struck a blow for the old amateur approach. Today, still not 50, he runs the whole of the world-wide Heinz organisation from headquarters in Pittsburgh, is also in his own right one of Ireland's most powerful and wealthy businessmen, and still plays rugby with the 'Golden Oldies'. Makes you sick really, but in spirit at least he is a man for the grey flannel bags held in place, I would like to hope, with his old Belvedere College tie.

Squash was still, just, a bit of an amateurs' game until recently. My wife's cousin whose wife's cousin was the British champion and got five Oxford blues without breaking sweat (squash, tennis, real tennis, fives, rackets I think – maybe ping-pong and jai alai as well for all I know) managed to combine squash and barristering to some effect. One day he was appearing in court at Southampton in the morning, changed on the train on his way to Wembley, and then beat one of the world's top players, a full-time professional Pakistani who had been practising and doing press-ups all week.

That won't happen again. It's all tracksuits and cheque books these days. There was a review in *The Times* the other day of the autobiography of Tony Lewis, sometime cricketer of Cambridge University, Glamorgan and England, now the cricket correspondent of the *Sunday Telegraph*, and a quintessential grey flannel bags man. 'Now,' said the reviewer, Ivo Tenant ('Ivo' is a good amateur's name), 'Lewis

would probably not gain a place at Cambridge. He would not choose
seven days a week professional cricket and the NUJ would object to
his joining the *Sunday Telegraph* without provincial experience.' True.

Now that we all wear the same uniform tracksuit, life is, of course,
fairer, less class conscious, better paid etcetera etcetera. All the same
I'm sad that the amateur has gone. I would love to think that a chap with
his grandfather's rackets and half a dozen initials before a double-barrelled
name might breeze into a Wimbledon final and demolish John McEnroe
in straight sets. Or that a working farmer might take time off from
bringing in the hay to go to the Oval and take all ten Australian wickets
for practically nothing. A pair of mildewed trousers held up with an
I Zingari tie, a harlequin cap and a baggy sweater, extravagant moustaches
and a private income were symbols, no doubt, of a terribly oppressive,
feudal society. But from where I sit on the boundary they still seem rather
fun.

4

Last Rites

GIVE ME THE MOONLIGHT

Sheila Fielding was quite definite about it. We might have been dancing together at the Tower Ballroom, New Brighton, for the sixth successive Saturday but that still didn't give me the right to circle my arm round her podgy waist on the walk back home. And what's more there was certainly not going to be any more kissing unless I kept my lips firmly closed.

Like many other female teenagers in the late Fifties (I'm thinking particularly of Pam Wilson, Carol Hodge and Jill Buxton), Sheila insisted upon being courted with mathematical precision. Stages of intimacy were calculated on a one to ten scale. Number One was 'holding hands' (although whether this included intertwining fingers depended on the occasion) while Number Two was 'kissing with tightly closed lips'. I won't go through all the other stages because obviously there were some personal and regional variations (girls in Chester, for example, were well known for not liking Number Four). It's probably quite enough to say that Number Ten – the end of the line unless one moved on to the engagement and marriage track – was nothing more erotic than 'hand on breast'. Not, it should be quickly emphasised, 'hand moving around on breast' but merely its static presence. (The finest practical demonstration of this courting move is to be found in the hotel scene in 'The Graduate' in which Dustin Hoffman suddenly shoots out a hand and plants it on Anne Bancroft's breast with all the aplomb of someone operating a sink plunger.)

It wasn't only action that you had to monitor. Words were equally significant. Persuading your partner to say they 'loved you' was a gruelling business: "Go on, say you love me." "No, why should I?" "Because you do a bit. I know you do." "How do you know?" And even when this was settled you were then immediately locked into an endless philosophical debate about the precise quality and quantity of the desired emotion. "But do you really love me?" "Yes, I do." "Really, really, really?" "Yes, I think so."

Often the frustration was intense, the anxieties intolerable. I can recall so many walks in the early morning when I was obsessed with the mistakes I'd made, mistakes like the one in August 1958 which lost me Iris Blanchard. It had been a good night up till the fateful moment. We'd seen a fine film (Burt Lancaster and Tony Curtis in 'The Sweet Smell of Success') and I decided that it was probably time to raise the romantic stakes a little. Once in her porch, I fixed Iris with what I took to be a Byronic

gaze and said in the most moving tone I could manage: "Iris, there's
something I want to say to you. I want you to know . . ." I searched my
brain for the most intense expression of my affection for her. "I want
you to know that there is no-one in the whole world I would rather say
goodnight to." I stood back to let the words sink in only to see her
take out her key, unlock the door, fire me one last look of disgust, and
then disappear. After such incidents it was no wonder that we all
rushed to welcome the naturalness of the Sixties with open arms.
Suddenly, it didn't matter what you did or said as long as it was
spontaneous and liberated. Everyone could do their own thing, could go
beyond Number Ten in a single evening without so much as a murmur
of complaint.

Only gradually did it become clear that the British were singularly
poor at being either natural or spontaneous. Maybe it was the lack of
Californian sunshine or the unsuitability of the British figure for the
average kaftan, but certainly most of us went on being as terrified of
touching each other as before, never felt quite certain what 'our thing'
was, and were in general about as laid back as Nelson's column.

And once old and young had abandoned the complex, hesitant,
stumbling routines and rituals of courting, there was no going back. Even
if we didn't feel in the least bit casual about what we now learned to call
'our relationship' with the other person, we had to do our damnedest
to pretend we were. The result was that we became not spontaneous and
natural but simply cavalier. The way we are today.

In fact, the essence of making out with other people these days is that
you must under no circumstances look as though you had any such
thing in mind. The name of the game is DRIFT. At a party or dance or
occasion, one merely drifts over the person who has caught one's
attention, drifts into conversation, and then without so much as a by
your leave drifts onto the dance floor and into a relationship.

Anyone nowadays who draws attention to what is going on by saying such things as, "Oh, I must say it is good to be dancing with you," or, "My word, I'm so glad I met you tonight," is automatically disqualified and will have to spend the last minutes of the evening helping the host and hostess to clear the ashtrays, or watching the band pack up their instruments.

Much the same languid routine is observed at the end of the affair. Indeed so casual are many disengagements that several of my friends often seem unable to answer such straightforward questions as, "Still going out with Sue?". They don't know for certain whether they are or not. There was none of this nonsense during the days of clumsy courting. Lovers never drifted away from each other like errant lilos: one of them 'chucked' the other. On occasions, of course, there was some dispute about who had chucked who (to this day I claim that I chucked Kate Lawley rather than the other way round) but absolutely no argument about whether or not the break had actually occurred. And once chucked, you stayed that way.

I only fully realised how far the world has moved on, how impossible it was to reverse the situation, when I was out dining in Soho a few weeks ago with an extremely elegant lady who had expressed a vague interest in publishing my next book. We had hardly been seated for a moment when she suddenly looked straight into my eyes and asked how I felt about some Number Two. I had a full five seconds of delighted nostalgia before I realised she was talking not about Closed Lip Kissing but the Won Tun soup.

AFTER THE FALL

My first wage packet in 1960 as a cub reporter was £5-a-week, from which, to my great chagrin, one shilling was deducted for income tax. Young journalists were paid according to age, and a colleague who had left school at 16 took home £3 16s 6d. I won't claim that we lived high on the hog, but I bought a perfectly serviceable motorbike for £30, which went forever on a gallon of petrol, costing – if memory serves me right – six shillings (30p).

It was about this time that Jimmy Hill, then leader of the professional footballers' union, succeeded in abolishing the maximum wage which stood at £19-a-week. Shortly thereafter – to the great astonishment of the public – Johnny Haynes, the England captain, became the first £5,000-a-year player. Jimmy Greaves, 'the prince of goal poachers', was sold to Italy for £100,000, for which now you would scarcely get two rooms in Clapham never mind a halfway to decent soccer player.

I was about to go to university, and looking ahead, £1,000-a-year was still a watershed salary which denoted achievement and offered security. I began what might loosely be called my 'serious' career on £750, as Britain revelled in the Profumo scandal. The rent on a small flat in Sheffield (with laundry), was £3-a-week, and four years later two rooms in Georgian Islington set me back a mere £9. I was by then working on Fleet Street, where I was paid £26-a-week.

In the West Riding of Yorkshire Chinese restaurants offered three-course lunches for 3/6d (17½p), for which today one would scarcely get a pat of butter. In Golders Green an Italian eatery served a set menu off white linen table-cloths for five bob. A stamp (class distinctions in postage lay in the future) was 1p – and I seem to remember that a letter got there the following morning; a quality newspaper cost little more. A decent pint of beer could be bought for two shillings (10p).

What concerns me now is not merely nostalgia. When I trot these figures out at the breakfast table, my children – employing broad, if somewhat dubious, northern accents – break into a chorus of 'when I were a lad, you could have a night out at the theatre, dinner for two, a cab home, and still have change from half-a-crown'.

My serious lament is for the freedom that a stable currency provided. I lost that first Fleet Street job; the paper went bust. But the local publican paid me what I had been earning as a reporter to work as a barman. I suffered no panic. When, shortly afterward I joined the *Observer*, senior journalists on the paper were getting well under £3,000-a-year.

93

There was no union; there didn't seem a need. Before the Sixties were
out, I had married and bought a house (admittedly requiring attention)
on the fringes of Chelsea for £8,000. We had a 100 per cent mortgage
at a fixed six per cent interest rate.

What such figures meant was that ambition could be channelled
towards what one wanted to do in the confidence that relatively modest
financial success would ensure comfort and security. The idea that a
bright young person might announce in all seriousness – as I heard one
such announce recently – that he could not afford to become a doctor
and was heading, therefore, to the City, would have seemed as unreal
as a Martian in the garden. Money, as ever, was essential, but it had not
become the boring preoccupation of these inflationary times.

The fall came, I believe, with decimalisation. Inflation, under
Chancellor Anthony Barber, was already roaring merrily along like a
hunt in full cry. By changing the currency, we changed the way we
thought about it: it was a subtle form of Orwellian 'double speak'. If
words don't retain their value, nothing else can. Abolishing the shilling
and the old penny was like ripping out a breakwater, leaving the tide free
to surge up the beach. I sometimes now translate present-day prices into
pre-fall £-s-d in order to keep alive some sense of the enormity of
inflation. A modest birthday card for a niece cost 13 shillings; the
wrapping paper to go with it was 15 bob!

By the mid-1970s I had some responsibility for recruiting journalists
to the *Observer*, and the people who came to see me were a very different
breed from my tyronic contemporaries and light years away in attitude
from the buccaneering figures of yesteryear. They arrived wearing suits,
and talked of mortgages; they were seeking a 'career', not a vocation.
They represented, I sensed gloomily, the future; their driving
motivation was not to perform, but to get ahead. In three years I never
sat eyeball-to-eyeball with an embryo James Cameron, but I detected plenty
of would-be Murdoch editors.

I lamented what I found, but I did not and still do not sit in judgment. There were no more £8,000 houses on the fringe of Chelsea (or anywhere else) to be had; the publican at the Cockpit had long since ceased to be a competitive employer with Fleet Street barons. The crystal ball was murky, but, with money leaking its value with what at times seemed South American rapidity, it was the careful men with the calculators to whom the brave new world belonged. A scribbler would remain, well, a scribbler. But the vista for the executive was lined with company cars, mobile phones, personal computers and Caribbean holidays.

What I perceived in my small corner was happening across the developed world. The Yuppy was born, and the wine bar and the manufacturers of Filofax were about to become the great beneficiaries. It was no longer what you did, but what you earned that counted; western civilisation had taken its first steps on the road that led to Ivan Boesky. The consequence was not only a two-tier society, the comfortable and the distinctly uncomfortable classes, but a distortion of human aspiration. 'Doing well' underwent a semantic sea change. The sale of books fell by 17 per cent in the years 1981 to 1987, while the import of BMWs clogged the docks.

I chanced the other night to hear a millionaire discussing his riches on the radio. He didn't, he said, value his fortune for its own sake, but it was 'drop dead' money. Now that he was affluent, he was free: he could happily tell others to drop dead and then go his own sweet way. When I were a lad, most of us had that freedom. It is for the lost liberty that I weep now into my £1.40 pint of beer.

SUNSET OVER TANKERTON

L ike John Masefield's sailor, I must go down to the sea again, to
the lonely sea and the sky, but I do not think I will ever go
down to the sea at Tankerton again for a summer holiday of the
kind I used to enjoy there as a very small boy in the 1930s.

I am told the name Tankerton originally meant a place where leather
tanners lived, but to me it encapsulated all the legendary magic of El
Dorado. In a sense, our summer holiday started months before we left

home, because every Sunday teatime my sister and I would carefully guide conversation towards this golden month to come. Would we stop for a picnic on the way – or should we drive straight there? Why did our mother insist we should never bathe on our first day by the sea, only on the second? What should we choose for a 'shivery bite', the name we gave to the biscuit or sandwich we always enjoyed after emerging from the sea literally shivering from the cold?

And then there was the drive itself. For this expedition, we hired an Armstong Siddeley from the Erith garage of McCluckie & Russell. Mr Russell dealt with customers at the pumps, while Mr McCluckie, a dour Scot, resplendent in a shiny peaked cap and an equally shiny blue suit, with black gloves, drove the car. The walls of their little office were decorated with prints by the motoring artist F. Gordon Crosby, showing great racing cars, and entitled 'The Endless Quest for Speed'. This quest did not concern us on our annual trip to Tankerton; Mr McCluckie proceeded with all the speed of a mourning car at a royal funeral.

Sometimes, my grandmother came with us. She was a Scottish lady of great age and determination, and insisted on bringing her bathchair, a curious three-wheeled contraption of varnished wicker with a long handle that extended from the front wheel to allow the occupant to steer. There was never a lack of men who could be hired to push them along the promenades of seaside towns in the 1930s. This chair was lashed to the car roof, to the intense mortification of my sister and I. Such was the simplicity of life in those days that, as we drove through Rochester and other towns on the way, and saw the reflection of this grotesque equipage in shop windows, people would cheer and clap, imagining we must be part of a travelling circus.

My parents and sister travelled in the rear compartment – one could not demean this area by calling it simply the back seat. Its roof was so high that, as Mr McCluckie regularly informed us with pride, it was possible to wear a top hat in his car, a hint that others of his clients were accustomed to doing so. Two tip-up seats faced a glass partition that properly divided the driver from the driven, above a clock with a silver face, a cut glass vase for flowers, and a rack of four pipes with a box of matches in a nickel case.

I preferred to eschew this luxury and sit up front with Mr McCluckie, where the smell of hot oil and burning paint was never far away. Control levers for altering the mixture of petrol and air to the carburettor and advancing or retarding the ignition sprouted like nickel-plated branches from the centre of the steering wheel; driving was a serious matter then, best left to professionals. The handbrake grew out of a generous hole in the floor boards. Looking down through this orifice, I could see the surface of the road unwind like a long grey ribbon.

We each occupied the same bedrooms every summer. One August, for reasons that now escape me, but which at the time seemed important, I removed a small picture from the wall of my bedroom, and twisted a penny until I had made a round hollow in the plaster behind it. In the following year, as the mail order advertisements like to say, 'in the privacy of my own room', I removed this picture again to see whether this hole was still there. It was – and some other similarly motivated occupant had embellished it with ears and hair and a big moustache.

The hall of the house was tiled in black and white squares. Sunshine through strips of bright blue and red glass around the front door bathed it in lurid light. From a hat peg on one wall hung fronds of seaweed, said to provide advance notice of changes in the weather by becoming damp, and dotted around the house postcards were pinned to doors with such admonitions as: 'Towels must not be hung out of windows', or 'Bathing costumes must not be wrung out in bathrooms'.

The first walk to the sea of each holiday was always something to remember, past a flag-pole where the town beadle, wearing a smart blue uniform, raised the Union Jack every morning and lowered it at dusk; in those days, the sun was never allowed to set on the flag. Then came the climb down wide steps cut into the cliff to a lower promenade, behind rows of huts. Each hut had a miniature verandah overlooking the sea, and inside a list of bye-laws was nailed on the back of the door: 'Commit no nuisance'; 'These premises are not to be occupied after dark'; 'Fires must not be lit'. How many negatives make one positive – and how many rules were made only to be disregarded?

Everyone seemed to own a spirit stove which was pumped until, with a roar, paraffin vapour took flame. We could brew tea, cook sausages and eat them on enamel plates provided, but somehow these activities, although involving flame, did not come within the category of fire. A bucket, discreetly hidden, stood behind a curtain for 'the slops' as tea leaves were called. As dusk rolled in over the beach, the men in each family, trousers rolled up to their knees, some still wearing on their heads a handkerchief, knotted in each corner as though against the heat of an expected midnight sun, carried these buckets to the water's edge and threw the contents into the tiny evening waves.

In my mind's eye I can still see this row of husbands silhouetted against the sea. Their children and grandchildren now disport themselves in the Seychelles, in Mauritius or Miami; they own villas and apartments in Spain and Portugal. But I wonder whether they and their families enjoy these holidays any more than we enjoyed the cramped quarters of our beach huts?

Days telescoped one into another with increasing speed. The sea that at first felt so cold that flesh literally crawled in protest, grew warmer; shingle so cruel initially became as friendly to the feet as the damp sand, ribbed by waves when the tide went out. Then, a single motor boat, moored far out at sea at high tide, lay on her side. By lifting a corner of a green tarpaulin that covered this craft, I could see the controls and the green-painted Morris marine engine. No craft has ever since held such attraction for me; in her were enshrined the wonders of all seven seas. And then came the last day, when the sun shone more brightly than on all preceding mornings. (Why did it never rain then, in those final hours of holiday? Or did it, but time has erased the memory?)

I would catch some shrimps and put them in my pail – metal in those days, no plastic, and decorated with pictures of jolly tars and starfish and capstans in bright colours, so soon to tarnish with the rust of winter.

All through the journey home I would keep a close eye on these shrimps, a last reminder of the holiday, an earnest of holidays to come, wedged between my feet in Mr McCluckie's car. But behind its proud radiator mascot of the inscrutable sphinx, the heat of that mighty engine dealt harshly with these little creatures. The water in the pail at the end of the journey was warmer than the Mediterranean, and the shrimps were dead. "You can't expect them to live outside their natural environment," Mr McCluckie would tell me in his strong Scottish accent. "In any case, nothing lives for long."

FOR WHOM THE BELLS TOLL

P erhaps the rot set in when the betrothal became an engagement. While the former is clearly defined as a contract or promise to marry another, the latter with its connotations of battles, appointments and employment, hints that unsullied connubial bliss is not necessarily assured. Perhaps it is unconscious recognition of this shift in meaning that has brought about the preparatory engagement.

It used to be simple: a couple announced their engagement, at which time the proposed date of the wedding was also mentioned, normally some six to twelve months hence. Not any more. Now we are forewarned that the engagement is to take place on some specified future date, but little mention is made of an actual marriage following on.

Having lobbed out a kettle for the pre-engagement, and a microwave with built-in browning facility for the engagement (the couple have been living together for five years anyway), the donor of these gifts is sometimes pleasantly surprised to discover that the wedding is not only going ahead, but even more astonished to discover that he is on the guest list – and not just as an also-ran. Having to winnow out numbers is not a modern dilemma, of course. In the 'Etiquette of Good Society', published in 1867, the parents of the bride-elect were advised to invite all friends who were not asked as guests, to witness the ceremony. A reasonable compromise, since the taking of vows is at the core of the proceedings.

My first intimation that times have changed occurred about seven years ago, when I received an engraved invitation for a wedding which apparently was to take place at 7 p.m. Slightly perplexed but bearing embroidered cotton percale duvet cover and pillow cases in hand, I arrived at the venue to discover that everything to do with the wedding, bar the shouting (literally), had already taken place. With ceremony long over, photographs taken, lunch eaten, speeches spoken, cake cut and champagne swilled, the final insult was having to buy my own drink from a bar flowing with whisky, but barren in ice – it was Suffolk, after all.

On the other hand, it is not just part-time invitees who need feel persecuted. For without a shot being fired, the 'professionals' have apparently usurped the role of the parents of the bride, and all must cower under their dictates. Take the photographer. Time was when a modest chap would arrive at the church with his Rolleiflex, eager to please and keen to cause the least inconvenience. It is true that granny's tulle-swirled hat would occasionally sprout a castellated hopper-head with matching drainpipe, but the autocratic photographers of today are not more proficient, just inordinately slower.

Not long ago I was at a wedding in Scotland where the unvictualled and parched guests were forced to loiter in the churchyard for at least an hour while the photographer bossily marshalled members of the bridal party into every conceivable permutation. If this inconsiderate practice is to continue, then I think the hosts are beholden to provide some sustenance. Waiting for the final group portrait, in which everyone, including any stray dog or gravedigger is included, would be marginally more tolerable if a tray or two of smoked salmon sandwiches and a few jugs of iced champagne were proffered to the bit-part players.

The tyrannical stills photographer has recently been joined by the video camera operator. Whilst acknowledging that the moving picture can add dramatically to fading recollections of the big event, I wonder how many guests remember that the pictures are accompanied by a sound-track? It is one thing quietly speculating with a confidante on the provenance of Aunt Hilda's lime-green crocheted suit with matching beret, but quite another to have this private interchange relayed to the assembled hordes (including Aunt Hilda) some hours later.

According to the editor of *Wedding and Home*, all brides want to have a wedding of unprecedented originality. They regale her with their dreams of arriving at the church in a carriage drawn by white horses, taking their vows in a hot-air balloon, or wearing a pre-Raphaelite wedding dress with a few lilies clutched loosely to their bosoms. Unfortunately, this 'originality' is shared by every bride alive.

Pointless to dwell on the countless unspeakable wedding breakfasts I have suffered, but an 'original' idea nowadays might be to appoint caterers who understand the difference between preparing food and manufacturing vulcanised chicken breasts, glistening with fake aspic and red pepper graffiti. The liberal dispensation of real champagne would not come amiss either, and I would advise impecunious hosts that if spumescent subterfuge is unavoidable, then a sparkling Saumur or Prosecco is infinitely more palatable than an Asti Spumante.

The final blow to my concept of the gentle wedding, is the introduction of the evening disco. The 'Etiquette of Good Society' sums up my feelings: 'Those guests who are not staying in the house should take their leave directly after departure of the happy couple. It is rather a tax upon the entertainers to provide amusements and keep the spirits of the party from flagging throughout this long, long day. The wisest thing is to send all the young people for a drive.' Quite.

. . . .

L loyd George did not know my father though it has to be said that Father was a great devotee of (and voter for) the Old Goat. I cannot imagine that LG had any greater admirer – certainly not among the male population. However, for my part I cannot claim to have reported on the great Welsh Wizard. He was slightly before my time as a journalist although I remember him and can quite vividly recall that majestic lilt coming over the wireless.

With one or two exceptions, of which more in a moment, I have had
to be content with lesser mortals among the prime ministers and political
leaders I have reported on at various points during the last 45 years or
so. From Clement Attlee and his remarkable team in that first post-war
Labour government through to the new world of John Major, the
cavalcade of change has been mind-boggling. Of course I am talking
about the scene as viewed from the ringside seat of a journalistic voyeur
and not about the relative policies or even politics of the great performers.
That old saw about politics being concerned with policies and not
personalities has never cut much ice with me.

My own reporting of the great theatre of political life started in the
age when it was quite essential (and not simply 'useful') to have a
shorthand note of never less than 120 words per minute and preferably
a good deal more than that. I am talking about the days before television,
before video, and even before tape recorders and microphones were
pushed under the nostrils of public figures and 'personalities'. The
word had to be recorded for posterity in Pitman's or Gregg's shorthand;
the gestures, the postures, the smile or the wince, the growl or the purr, the
fortissimo cry or the stealthy whisper was described with a writing style
that has seemingly gone out of fashion in daily journalism. Nowadays
everything is 'recorded' rather than reported. Moreover, it is the visual
impact of public affairs rather than the written epic which captures
moments of contemporary history for posterity to contemplate if it should
ever choose so to do.

I do not say that the written record has disappeared altogether nor
that no reporter uses any shorthand at all; it is not yet quite that cataclysmic.
But we are all aware of the inescapable trend. Go to any major political
convention these days and you will rarely see what we used to call 'the
Press tables'; the trestled working-posts for an army of reporters with
notebooks, even pencils, armed only with a good ear and a shorthand note
plus, to be sure, a marvellous eye for the unorthodox. Now it's virtually

all electronic and the great performers, regardless of party or policies, walk onto the stage of the prepared theatre to do their party piece. Down in the amphitheatre there are the lights, mile upon mile of cable, men (and women, usually extremely glamorous women too) with clipboards, mobile phones, stems of sound-equipment devices which look like remote control rods for cleaning cars and an entire armoury of electronic gear hanging about their flak jackets and jeans; it is, I have often felt, an invasion from another planet of media, stamping over the personalities, as well as the policies, or whatever else lies in their path.

What worries me most about all this panoply of change is not so much the elimination of those old skills of shorthand and what I call person-to-person reporting but, much more, the effect it has had, and is having on our public figures. One must ask, just how much was Margaret Thatcher moulded by the age of television and electronic communication – rather than her influencing it? What are we to expect from John Major or Neil Kinnock or Paddy Ashdown et al?

When I reflect on how my generation of journalists reported on and described the qualities (or otherwise) of Clem Attlee, Ernest Bevin, Winston Churchill, Anthony Eden, RAB Butler, Harold Macmillan, Aneurin Bevan, Alec Douglas-Home, Harold Wilson and so on, I simply cannot begin to imagine how they would have handled the modern image-makers. It is true that television began to make its real impact on political life during the premiership of Harold Macmillan and was well into its groove by the time Harold Wilson came into office. Yet I recall the general election campaign of 1964 which I reported for the *Daily Herald*. My role was to spend the whole campaign reporting Wilson, and apart from the BBC sound recording equipment I do not offhand remember any reporter with a tape recorder in his knapsack. Even the television cameras then had their work cut out to try to keep abreast of notebook-carrying reporters. As for the greatest orators of them all – Lloyd George apart, of course – Winston Churchill and Aneurin Bevan

. . . well, Heaven knows how they would have coped with the cameras and the cables, the clipboard armies, the make-up parlours and the microphones stuffed into their faces. Bevan would have exploded with a terrible wrath and Winston, I fancy, would have growled an expletive that might well have shocked even the most glamorous of the clipboard, microphone-thrusting beauties who flicker behind, and oft-times onto, our TV screens. Harold Macmillan would surely have dropped the family silver.

I still have my shorthand notes from Attlee, Churchill, Macmillan, Nye Bevan, Wilson, Callaghan . . . but alas, I've lost my treasured attempted shorthand note of Ernest Bevin. As Foreign Secretary the great, trundling figure of Bevin would mount the platform, or whatever, and start his speech with a sentence which never finished. There were no commas, no full stops, no punctuation. It simply went on, across the world, from Stalin to Truman and back again while the struggling hacks sweated and frowned over their Pitman's. I wish now that I could have had a tape recorder then. I miss those marvellous old days of reporting in the raw; I must admit, there were moments when the old system did have its profound limitations.

. . . .

A DREAM OF COFFEE DREGS

C offee, Sirs, has been the Salvation of this Nation. If t'were not for the genteel and salubrious Effects of the Coffee Houfes we would affuredly be a City of Drunkards. Was it not the general Cuftom among us, even when I was a Boy, that no *Bargain* could be drove or *Commerce* conducted but it must be tranfacted at a Tavern, and were not Men's Wits scrambl'd by continual draughts of Ale or Wine 'til they forgot what Bufiness they were come for? Now

Gentlemen conduct their Affairs over a Dish or two of Coffee then go their way as sprightly as you like. I know not if Coffee make Politicians wife, as Mr Pope says in his excellent Satire (*The Rape of the Lock – Ed*), but I vouch that it makes our Merchants prudent.

'Tis not to say that Coffee is a Nostrum for all our Ills. To speak plain I never did account those magick Properties to Coffee that are advertifed by Quacks and Charlatans: the Cure of Dropsy, if you pleafe, or the Rheum or Gout! I wager my last Sovereign that these miraculous Cures were accomplifh'd after a twelve-hour in the Ale-House. Melancholy of the Head excites in Men imaginings of fatal Humours, for which Apothecaries but Prefcribe a Pennyworth of Coffee as Physic. But should I complain? *Bufiness is Bufiness*, as my friend Jacob says moft wittily.

But to the Point, Sirs. Yefternight I had a dream wherein methought I was tranfported beyond my mortal Span some three hundred Years. I could recount to you Wonders reveal'd to me that if I spoke of them you would have me locked up in Bedlam for an incurable Dolt. But you shall hear of my bootless Quest for the bitter Berry, that innocent Bev'rage: item, an honest Pot of Coffee, in the Year of our Grace MCMLXXXVIII.

Enquiring of a fellow where Coffee might be sold I was directed in my Dream to the *Signe of Ye Sandwich Bar*, a mean and narrow Shoppe that had none of the Comforts of a Coffee House where a man might spend an Hour or Two in Diverfion. In truth it was a dreary Place where no man tarried, but straightway took his Bev'rage out with him. Never did I see such *Hocus-Pocus* to fill a Dish with Coffee! Such a mighty Engine was engaged for this Purpose, adorned by Handles, Spouts and divers Pipes to summon up a Steaming and Hiffing as t'were all *the Serpents of Hell* had been unleafh'd. To what end I know not save to agitate the fuming Liquor with foamy Bubbles that affix'd themfelves when supped to the upper Lip. It seems it is a forme of Coffee named after the *Capuchins*, and the terrible Engine a Christian form of Torture to convert the infidel Bean!

So I ventured abroad to see what other Barbarities they wreaked upon the fragrant Bean of Araby, and anon I came upon a throng of People around a wooden Booth where victuals call'd *Snax* (which we call Meat Pies) were sold. Drawing near I obferv'd how the Hawker served his manner of Coffee: firft is meafured into a parchment cup a fine brown Powder and mix'd with scalding Water. Then is added another Powder, white and granular, which did discolor the whole Complexion of the Bev'rage. When I enquired if those were *Epsom Salts* – which are become the Rage of late with constipat'd Gentlefolk – he appeared mightily amufed. 'Tis Milk' says he. 'Forsooth' say I, 'a terrible Drought indeed that so dessicates the Cows that they give forth white Powder!' which did amufe him more mightily still.

How tafted this wonderful Potion, you ask Sirs? Why, if you had boil'd the muddy effufions of the Fleet and serv'd it in the name of Coffee, it would by Comparifon have smelt fairer, looked more wholefome, tafted less noxious and been no worse an Affront to the Stomack withal. Faith, if I had serv'd such *counterfeit Coffee*, I would have long been in the Poor House.

Here's another Odditie. They have in certain Places where men forgather in great numbers, publick *Fountains of Coffee* which, upon the Application of a Token, gush forth in meafured Stream. Ay, and Tea and Chockolat whichsoever you desire. I know not what Alchemie is employ'd within, but 'tis paffing strange: there is not one jot of diff'rence betwixt them. Is this to be the Fate of our Country, that it knows not, nor cares not, what it drinks?

Such was the headlong Rush of Life, as I obferv'd, that even their Coffee must needs be Instant or *Expresso*, or else macerat'd into Effence, or dried by freezing (t'was thus advertifed!), or wrapp'd in Bags to make infufions. They have grown paffing indiff'rent to their Palates, 111

· ·

else why would they engage Garblers (*official purifiers – Ed*) to expurgate that part of it they call *Caffeyne*, or wish to add an Elixir which by its Appellation doth promife Long Life?

But stay – I had almost wearied of finding a Coffee House when I chanced upon an Establifhment called a *Café*, which I was affured was French for Coffee. Here at length I might idle away the hours over a Dish of Coffee in civil Companie, savour the roast'd Perfumes, smoak a pipe or two and put the World to rights. The pot-boy served a curious dish of Coffee in a moft ingenious Dish with a loop'd Handle wherein to insert the Finger. To what a Pitch of Perfection is Civilifation come! I then bade him bring me a selection of Churchwardens and a Box of his best Tobacco, but the impudent Fellow shook his Head and address'd me to a Notice on the Wall. No Smoaking. God preferve us from these Frenchified fashions!

Such, Sirs, was my Dream, and never was I more reliev'd to wake and find it so. For if t'were true in its particulars, what Destiny awaits these Sanctuaries of Temperance and Frugality and good Society, our Coffee Houses? We shall all be out of Bufiness, and the Name of Lloyd's pass from the Memory!

· ·

Editor's note: Edward Lloyd was the proprietor of Lloyd's Coffee House in 1688, from which the present international insurance market is descended. This In Memoriam mysteriously appeared at Lime Street, in time to be published in the special tercentenary issue of Lloyd's Log.

5

Places in Time

FAREWELL TO FULLERS

They exist still, of course, at our more colonnaded resorts and as
outposts of Englishness in such far-flung spots as Cairo and
Rome. But tea shops are not what they were – nor, for the most
part, even where they were, having been replaced by something
smelling of fried onions behind a plastic facia. The death rattle sounds
for the Copper Kettle.

114   Unless you wish to pay through the nose in a hotel lobby, it is

practically impossible to get a cup of tea in London any more. Tastes change, we are to believe: the English have gone pagan and relinquished their afternoon rite of passing round thin bone china and the even thinner cucumber sandwiches. But you cannot get a cup of coffee either, not without an accompaniment of burger and chips ('No beverages served on their own' advises my local fast food outlet where Fullers Tea Rooms once stood). New York is your best bet for an authentic English muffin. The tea shop dispensed all three, according to the hour – coffee and biscuits for the morning shopping crowd, then the switch to tea and out with the toasting fork immediately after 'businessmen's light lunches 12.00–2.00'.

Our corporate fading image of tea shops gone by is almost a pastoral, Merrie England one – tea shoppes rather than tea shops, with Betjemanesque names like The Spinning Wheel or Dorothy's Pantry, run by two maiden ladies in lilac smocks (one of them being presumably Dorothy – did they toss a coin to decide whose name would be immortalised in pokerwork?) serving scones and fancies at dark oak tables amid a clutter of Benaresware. Or, especially among city-dwellers, it is an Edwardian clerk's-eye-view memory of clattering tea rooms with steamed-up windows – Lyons or the ABC (the splendidly-named Aerated Bread Company) where old gaffers sat mumbling to themselves at the marble tables, and there was always a sodden newsvendor garlanded with a hessian sack of buff *Posts* or *Echoes*, tallying up his Late Final takings over beans on toast.

In fact, between plebeian Joe Lyons and the genteel Dorothy, there ranged a whole spectrum of different types and standards of tea shop, as distinct in tone from one another as, let us say, McDonald's, Spud-U-Like and Pizza Express which have now replaced them in the public's affection. As an office boy roaming the streets of Leeds with an unquenchable appetite for toasted teacakes, on which I lived almost exclusively, I had a choice of a good dozen shops and tea rooms of

115

varying quality which I would frequent at least three times a day, going upmarket or downmarket according to the state of my finances.

For 'elevenses' – an official 20-minute break, subsidised, in those paternalistic days, by a sixpence-a-day allowance out of the petty cash – I would resort to the Kismet Café, a mock-Gothic establishment in the basement of a block of sooty commercial chambers, where the tables were marked out as chessboards and you could indulge your Grand Master fantasies for the price of a milky coffee. Looking back on that scene, with pipe-puffing managing clerks in funeral suits and celluloid collars twinkling over their half-moon spectacles as they checkmated their inky juniors in the time it took to get through a plate of chocolate digestive biscuits, I have the unreal impression of having once lived inside a novel by Arnold Bennett.

Lunch would be taken either at a Lyons – we had three, all self-service (how I envied cosmopolitan London Lyonisers who, legend had it, were served in Palm Court surroundings by saucy 'Nippies' in frilly cap and apron; I pined to live in the capital solely to be able to scoff my toasted teacakes in a Corner House to the strains of a string quartet) – or at the Dairies across the street from the office. The Dairies was one of those local bakery chains which then flourished in most big towns and which happily still do in some. Cake shop in front, café in the back. Welsh rarebits and a scalding stainless steel teapot that could take the skin off your fingers. And puppy-fat-plump waitresses for office boys to fall in love with.

Afternoon tea – unlike 'elevenses' not a ritual sanctioned by my employers but snatched under the guise of running errands – might sophisticatedly be taken in one of the department store restaurants where, the air still heady with the aroma of lunchtime haddock, mannequins would pirouette from table to table – I prayed they would not stop at mine – showing off the season's frocks for the mature figure. Or, if even more in funds (a Bon Marché 'set tea' was not for those on a tight budget), there was a superior, Kardomah-type café much frequented by lady shoppers from Harrogate, which cut its sandwiches into triangles and its toast into fingers.

Otherwise there was always the Dairies again for another round of badinage; or there were the plush cinema cafés – though these I liked to reserve for high tea of poached egg on toast on red-letter evenings; or there were the milk bars, all chrome, white tiles and glass. Milk bars, I realise, are a far cry from tea shops; but you could get a cup of tea in them, which is more than can be said for the kebab joints which have taken their place. And if you were feeling really orthodox, there was always the authentic Tudor Tea Shoppe, that is, not authentic Tudor – a little bit of Stratford-on-Avon hard by the corporation slaughterhouse.

All gone now, there and elsewhere. Junk food, the rates, and the reluctance of ladies to don lilac nylon habits and take vows of chastity to a plate of Eccles cakes, have all taken their toll. As has the British horror – bizarre in a nation which imagines itself to be steeped in tradition – of appearing old-fashioned. Our tea shops have gone the way of our chop houses and our Victorian gin palaces in the interests of getting up-to-date, not being left behind by progress, and all the rest of it. We must be the only nation in the world, bar Pol Pot Cambodia, to have deliberately set about wiping its traditional eating places off the map.

What would happen, I wonder, if a Texas go-getter stormed over here selling poached-egg-on-toast franchises? We should probably finish up with a nationwide chain of Dorothy's Pantries, all with identical thatched roofs and chintz curtained bow windows, and all making money hand over fist. Meanwhile: stands the church clock at ten to three, and is there honey still for tea? No.

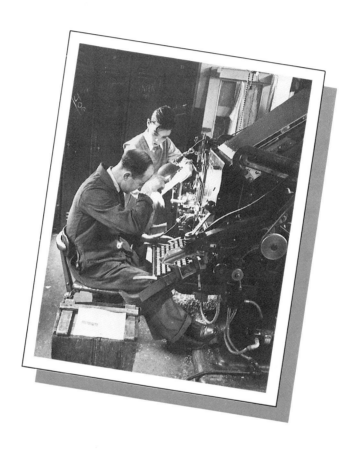

O nce upon a time there was a place in London called The Street of Adventure. It produced newspapers and magazines that reflected life in Britain and the great wide world outside. It employed journalists who not only reported what the prime minister said in parliament yesterday but who lifted the reader out of his mundane existence in Metroland and took him on a raft down the Amazon, up Everest with Hillary, or round the Horn with Chichester.

To work there you had to be one of the best, and the ambition of every junior reporter on the *Northern Echo* or the *Adelaide Advertiser* was one day to make it to Fleet Street. True, many of those who did find jobs there found that reporting the Law Courts in London was not much different from reporting the magistrates' court in Carlisle. But as they got off the Number 13 bus at Fetter Lane and walked down the Street there was always a thrill of the unexpected that only an industry as instant and as ephemeral as newspapers can produce.

Take a young South African journalist called O. D. Gallagher who got a job on the *Daily Express* in the 1930s. He wandered into the newsroom after a boring morning reporting a singing dog in Croydon. The foreign news editor saw him and said, "I want you to go to Abyssinia. There seems to be a war going on there. Pick up some money from cashiers – I suggest you take some of it in gold – and catch the night ferry." And he was away.

Gallagher went on to report the war, met Evelyn Waugh and became a character in 'Scoop'. From Abyssinia he went to Spain for the Civil War, met Hemingway and Robert Capa, moved on to Shanghai for the fighting between the Chinese and Japanese, raced back to France for the opening shots of the Second World War, covered the Battle of Britain, flew off to Singapore and got himself sunk along with the Repulse and the Prince of Wales and then made it to Burma just in time to get out again at bayonet's length ahead of the Japanese.

And all the while Gallagher's readers were with him; watching Franco's troops march into Madrid; tapping out an obituary for the *Daily Telegraph*'s correspondent shot dead in the Battle of Shanghai; counting downed German bombers in the home counties; up to his neck in oil in the Gulf of Siam; typing a dispatch by the light of blazing Rangoon. Someone else could do the analysis, the explanation of what it all meant. Gallagher told us what it was like to be there: life and death and history in the making.

119

It is hard to pinpoint just when Fleet Street began to die. It was probably when larger-than-life proprietors like Beaverbrook and Northcliffe went and the money-men began to take over. The old proprietors did not run Fleet Street mainly to make money; they did it for the power and the glory. The faceless accountants failed to see why O. D. Gallaghers should charter planes to Singapore when there were perfectly adequate reports available from the wire services or some underpaid local correspondent.

Improved communications, a shrinking global electronics village in which television could show you what was happening 5,000 miles away before your own correspondent could get to Heathrow, made the accountants' demands hard to resist.

New technology was the final blow. The old printing system – hot metal and slow presses – meant that newspapers had to be strategically placed: close to a railway terminal for country-wide distribution, and close to the City centre so that the vans could get the papers around the capital's breakfast tables. And where the printers had to be, the journalists had to follow, for in the old days the copy went from journalist to composing room by hand.

But the new technology, born of the computer age, broke the link between the printing process and the journalist. Now an editorial staff can create a newspaper and feed it to presses anywhere in the country down a telephone line. (Some younger journalists have never seen a printing press, let alone met a printer.) With no longer any need for his newspaper to be centrally located, the new-wave newspaper proprietor could not wait to sell his expensive real estate and go elsewhere – Wapping, the Isle of Dogs, Battersea.

This may have been fine for profits but it was death to Fleet Street and the journalism it represented. Old Fleet Street journalists were sociable characters who mixed with the people they wrote about. They entertained them in the pubs around the Street; they took them to lunch; they invited them to the newspaper office. In those days Fleet Street at lunchtime was full of the hubbub of tomorrow's news in the making.

But who wants to travel to Wapping to meet a reporter? What reporter wants to pop up from the Isle of Dogs for a quick drink in Soho to see an informant? Who's going to make the journey from Battersea for a bit of gossip with another journalist? So the news is gathered on the telephone and from the television screen, the background filled in from a databank, and a new generation of journalists interview and write about people they never meet.

And since the scattering of their papers, they do not even meet each other much any more. The gossip, the discussion, the argument, the exchange of information that is such an important part in helping a writer form a view that will add dimension to his reporting is gone. The pubs of Fleet Street have been taken over by lawyers and money dealers, the cafés and little restaurants replaced by cut price electronics shops. It is now a tacky, dirty little street that joins Aldwych and Ludgate Circus.

And with its demise went the sense of adventure that was a vital part of its spirit. As today's young reporter ploughs through Docklands traffic to his aseptic open-plan office he does not dream that he might soon be on his way to join an expedition to the heartland of New Guinea. He knows exactly where he will spend the rest of the day – in front of his VDU.

SAILING INTO THE SUNSET

On Friday 12 August 1977, I was out in a small sailing-boat, lazily approaching the Needles Channel at the western end of the Isle of Wight. In the middle distance we spotted a ship. She was more graceful than the commonplace tankers and ferries littering the Solent approaches; after a few moments, I caught through the binoculars the distinctive pale lilac gleam of her hull, and knew her for a mail-ship of the Union Castle line. She would be outward bound for the Canaries and the Cape, with cargo and mail in the hold, and the passengers lining the rail to listen to the band and see the shores of England drop below the horizon. So we pulled our mainsail down and drifted, watching her out of sight. A last glitter of sunlight picked out her white superstructure, and she was gone.

It was a moment of peculiar poignancy, as every great liner's departure always is; but I am glad I did not know at that moment how poignant it was. If I had, I would probably have wept. For it was when we reached Southampton next day, and read the local paper, that we realised what we had actually seen. The *Windsor Castle*, last of the mail-ships, had set out for Cape Town on the last outward sailing by a British liner; a whole way of life had vanished over the horizon with her. Her sister ships were already gone, ingloriously sold or broken up; the mail contract was ended. Oil prices, rising wages and the advent of huge container ships had ruined business. Union Castle, after 120 years, was the last of the great companies to pull out of an honourable old trade which had become impossible. Sea travel was dead.

Of course, you can still go on a cruise. You can still lean on the rail of a ship and watch the wake; rise at dawn and share the stillness of the morning watch with the crew, and wander out after dinner on to a swaying boat deck to gaze at the moon. But it will never be the same. Cruise ships are out on the water entirely for your pleasure; they are empty of cargo and full of what the brochures call 'recreational facilities'; if they go to Piraeus, or Barbados, it is only to humour you, not to deliver anything. The old mail-ships ran to a schedule, all year round, in all weathers. Passengers were looked after, but kept in their place; and when you docked in Zanzibar or Aden, there were cargoes to be loaded, as well as sightseeing buses to book. At least half your fellow-passengers would not be doing the trip for pure holiday pleasure; they would be on business, or emigrating. It all conspired to give sea travel a unique dignity and purpose; in richness and complexity   123 and seriousness, a real sea journey is as different from a 'cruise' as a grandfather clock is different from a quartz and plastic watch.

I was lucky, I just caught the end of this great era. My father was a diplomat, and as a small child I travelled out to the Far East and back on P&O liners. Later, I had the opportunity to develop hopeless teenage crushes on the resplendent officers on two Union Castle ships, the *Pendennis Castle* on the trip out to South Africa, and the *Braemar Castle* on the five-week journey back up the east coast and through the Suez Canal. I remember particularly a long-suffering second engineer (I knew all the stripes on their sleeves, generally, by the end of the first day out; the company gave you a chart). I used to mooch around the boat deck at dusk, kicking deck quoits and looking soulful, while the poor man tried to smoke a quiet pipe before his evening watch.

Apart from falling in love with the officers there were wonderful ways to spend time on these ships. You could swim in the pool, a particularly novel experience on rough days before stabilisers were fitted, as the water slopped excitingly from side to side and occasionally soaked the poolside deck chairs (whereon they would let a bit more water out, until we children splashed and shrieked in an echoing tiled cavern). You could walk eight times round the deck, which was rumoured to be an exact mile. You could play games with various flat objects guaranteed not to roll overboard – rubber deck quoits, tarry rope rings, odd-looking hockey-pushers with which you played a form of giant shove-ha'penny. You could sit in the quiet little ship's library and read old detective stories from the diamond-paned glass bookcases; or you could work furiously on your eyecatching costume for the fancy dress gala night. Someone always came as the Captain, having purloined the assistant purser's spare white hat. Without videos or discothèques or over-frequent cruisey harbour stops, we were thrown back on simple amusements.

As for the evenings, *Pendennis Castle* with 800 passengers was pretty sophisticated. There were generally at least two kinds of dancing every night, and a good few film shows. The *Braemar Castle*, which brought us home by the slow eastern route, was a one-class ship with a comparatively tiny complement of passengers, and had to be more ingenious. Every few nights for five whole weeks the purser would devise some wild diversion. It might be fancy dress; it might be more obscure, like Frog Racing, a curious parlour game unique to liners, which involved much horseplay by the larkier young officers and a race-card filled with horribly punning names like Sex Kitten, by Awful Mistake, out of Ship's Cat. There were concerts, particularly if some distinguished musician had been incautious enough to put his real name on the passenger-list. There was the Talent Contest, which made the ship's lounge into one of the last places on earth, probably, where you were likely to hear someone stand up and recite 'The Green Eye of the Little Yellow God'. There was the Crossing The Line ceremony, with Neptune in a green seaweed beard, and some poor devil being plastered in shaving-foam and thrown into the pool.

And all the time, there was the sea itself; our supporting element, our cradle by night, our galloping steed by day. Exciting as it was to make a new port, to smell the hot spicy land and watch the men and the cranes unloading crates and bales onto a foreign quay, I remember too the way my heart lifted every time we set to sea again; once more a self-contained, purposeful, disciplined world free from the clutter and complication of harbour. Despite all the horseplay, there was a seriousness about it; this, for the moment, was our ship, and even though we were passengers, we shared some of the dignity of the seafarer, because we shared his risk. On the last journey of the last mail-ship Colonel Laurens van der Post said: "For some years I have had a nightmare that this kind of travel, this kind of ship we are sailing in might be abolished, and I've just since Las Palmas woken up and found that indeed this is so. I wonder if we realise what precisely is being taken away from us . . . what is coming to an end is not just the Union Castle line, but a great era in human history which started with the Renaissance, which started in an age of discovery and adventure, to find new nations and new lands."

Well, it is all over now. What happened to those ships? I can hardly bear to tell you. *Pendennis Castle* nearly became a floating casino in Hong Kong, but was broken up instead. Poor little *Braemar Castle* has been scrap for 20 years; and *Windsor Castle* ended up in Jeddah as an 'accommodation base and leisure centre' with artificial grass and palm trees on her decks. Still, she is in one piece. I might go and see her one day; stand on deck, shut my eyes, and vainly hope to feel her lift to a wave, or to smell the first cinnamon breeze blowing offshore from Zanzibar.

SOHO, SO LONG, SO SAD

S oho is dying. She lingers on doggedly but she has been a terminal case ever since the day Lord Wolfenden published his report which drove prostitutes from the streets. In their place there sprung up the industry of pornography. Dirty bookshops, blue cinemas and strip clubs, and in very nearly every instance where they now stand there was once a café, bistro, restaurant or delicatessen. Now it is only the 127 pornographers who can afford to pay the rents and rates of these once delightful premises.

The decline of the quality of life has really taken a fancy to dear old Soho. I first came to Soho in 1948 when I was 16 years old. It was love at first sight. I became immediately addicted. My brother was a student at St Martin's School of Art at the time and one day he asked me up there to meet him in the café where the students had their coffee breaks. I thought I was in Disneyland after two fairly disastrous years in a strict public school. The Swiss Café, as it was known, was in Manette Street by the side of Foyles. I found myself in the midst of would-be poets and painters, writers, layabouts, café philosophers, bums, a few genuine Bohemians, a vanished breed, actors and some very pretty girls.

It represented everything I was brought up to think was wicked so, of course, it was magic. I was introduced to sex, drinking and horse racing in no time at all. Yes, 1948 was a very heady year. As time went by and I became less socially gauche I spread my wings and got to know the Soho beyond Manette Street. Soho proper was and is enclosed by Oxford Street, Charing Cross Road, Shaftesbury Avenue and Berwick Street market. In Dean Street the York Minster (sometimes known as the French) had a genuine feel of Parisian café society. In the morning the local tradesmen and shopkeepers plus the mostly French prostitutes who Wolfenden thought so outrageous would come in, sip the Amer Picon or Ricard and chat and gossip and discuss the village of Soho.

It was charming. The French girls were elegant, polite, bought their round and never solicited for custom. Madame Valerie who owned the patisserie around the corner – still there – held court and poured great quantities of Guinness into her gigantic body. Later on, and for quite a while, I would have a routine drink every morning with Dylan Thomas who was usually a bit hungover. Nice man sober, impossible drunk. But

most of the poets and writers used the Highlander further up the street.
And what a different bunch they were to the mostly awful advertising
yuppies who use it now. Apart from Dylan there was Louis McNeice,
George Barker, John Heath-Stubbs, David Wright – I can't remember
them all, but it was a who's who of modern poets. Then there were the
painters Roberts Colquhoun and McBryde, John Minton, Lucian Freud,
Keith Vaughan, Francis Bacon – not a millionaire then – all of them now
represented in the Tate.

Such people intermingled with a very different bunch who could have
come straight out of William Saroyan. Ironfoot Jack, Handbag Johnny, Sid
the Swimmer and The Fox. The one place they couldn't get into though
was the slightly exclusive Gargoyle Club on the corner of Meard Street.
It was a beautiful place and the interior had been designed by Matisse.
It was a bit up-market but they put up with what were then Bohemians.
On a good night it was fascinating to see people like Robert Newton
ranting and roaring into the early hours. After that it was across the
road to recover at an all-night coffee stall on what was then a bombed
site. Gaston Berlemont, the guvnor of the French pub, said that the fire
which destroyed the wine merchant there had improved some wine found
still intact in the cellar by years.

I worked as a navvy building the block which replaced it and
customers from the French would sometimes pass a glass of Pernod to
me over the wall to the intense annoyance of the site foreman. But I could
still keep in touch with all these people even when doing nasty jobs. I
worked for a while as a dish washer in the famous Mandrake Club in
Meard Street.

The Mandrake started out as a chess club with coffee only in a
one-roomed cellar. Boris Watson, the enormous Russian with an
uncertain temper who owned it, reputedly killed one of his customers in
his previous club, the notorious Coffee Ann. Eventually he was granted a
licence and expanded the club to a further six cellars so that it extended

129

right under Dean Street. I would collect my wages there and move immediately into the bar to spend them in company with some legendary Fleet Street men like Cyril Connolly, Maurice Richardson and John Davenport.

A few yards away there was the famous Colony Room Club known to all as Muriel's. It is still there but Muriel who held court is dead and the place has gone to seed. It was oddly enough a rather smart club then and expensive for its time. Muriel only really liked famous and rich people in there and I think she allowed me in there because I could make her laugh. And what an odd assorted bunch it used it. It was largely a homosexuals' watering hole and I have drunk with Noel Coward, E. M. Forster and Tom Driberg in there. More recently the Kray twins used it. Strangely enough they were social climbers and they tried to climb by giving money to charities. I didn't realise who they were when I first met them and was rather rude to Ronnie. I sometimes wonder how I am still alive.

But Soho was never as full of villains as the Sunday papers made out. The famous knife fight between Jack Spot and Italian Albert Dimes was strictly personal, as was the shooting dead of Tony Muller by a friend. What I mean is that they represented no threat to the likes of you and I or a passing tourist.

Being flat broke in those days, the one thing I didn't get many helpings of was the great food that abounded in Soho. The generosity of friends gave me glimpses of it though. The best restaurant I could eat frequently in was the upstairs restaurant at the French pub. Never mind the atmosphere downstairs, upstairs you could believe you were in Paris. It was all of £1 5s for an excellent three course meal and a bottle of good wine. They had a nutty waiter there too who thought he was a good spoof player and he would like to play you double or quits for the bill. I am glad I was streetwise by then.

130   What is awful is that more than half the people I have mentioned

here are now dead. I fear Soho will follow shortly. Now I sit and tipple in the Coach and Horses or the Groucho Club and think that most clichés have an element of truth about them. They were indeed the 'good old days'.

It was an improbable discovery. There they still were, these brazen
imperial relics, scattered at intervals across the parkland of the
Calcutta maidan. Sixteen statues memorialising the British Raj,
undisturbed by either politicians or vandals a couple of decades after
India had achieved independence from the foreign rule. Here were
viceroys and commanders-in-chief, superior aliens all, including the
6th Earl of Mayo, trotting on his charger at a crossroads in the park.

132

The inscription across the plinth referred to His Lordship as 'Humane, Courteous, Resolute and Enlightened. Struck down in the midst of a Patriotic and Beneficent Career on 18th February 1872 by the treacherous hand of an assassin. The People of India, mourning and indignant, raise this statue.' Where on earth in the old colonial world apart from here, I wondered then, would you find such an endearing tolerance? The answer, I have long since realised, is nowhere else at all.

That was nearly 20 years ago, and I was seeing India for the first time, astonished by many indigenous things, but by none more than the native capacity to live amiably with an often disagreeable past. It gradually dawned on me that the peculiar genius of the great sub-continent is to absorb its history swiftly, to see even in the bleaker episodes of not so long ago patterns that can enrich the present: a talent which, in part, makes for a civilisation.

Throughout India and Pakistan today the marks left by various invaders are familiar features in every town, as much of a local motif as the Roman foundations, Norman churches and Scandinavian place names that litter the British Isles. I have detected 'Liberté, Egalité, Fraternité' upon the stucco of what was once l'Hôtel de Ville, just a few miles up the Hooghly from Calcutta, residue of what was (until 1951) the tiny French colony of Chandernagore. On the other side of the country to the west, in the main square of Panjim, a monument still stands to an expatriate da Silva, who owes this prominence to the fact that the Portuguese ruled Goa until 1961. Second only to the Mughal heirlooms, however, the mementoes of the British are the imperial remains that chiefly catch the eye. Buildings most of all, of course.

There must be hundreds of these, possibly thousands, quite apart from the Lutyens extravaganza in New Delhi, home for the last five viceroys and since then the residence of Indian presidents (two-thirds of a mile round the foundations, which makes it bigger than Louis XIV's palace at Versailles). The building above all others that I fell for before long was that preposterous Victoria Terminus in Bombay, a crocketed, gargoyled, traceried and vaulted neo-gothic folly of a railway station, a sort of St Pancras-by-the-Ghats. But there are daintier period survivals as well, like St Mary's Church in Madras, where Robert Clive married Margaret Maskelyne in 1753; and Christ Church, Simla, whose chancel frescoes were painted by Rudyard Kipling's father, Lockwood.

Not so long ago I was introduced to the officers' mess of the Chitral Scouts, high up on Pakistan's north-west frontier, and found myself peering at photographs of Britons on its walls, men who had led the Scouts until a generation ago, some of whom still exchange Christmas cards with their Muslim successors. And perhaps it was Captain H. de C. O'Grady, with the clipped moustache and crinkled hair, first commanding officer in 1903, who chose the Royal Stuart tartan which the pipe band of the Scouts continues to wear on ceremonial occasions in that wild and belligerent place.

I am still surprised by the care with which the military connection is tended, when I remember that British soldiers were on the sub-continent for the sole purpose of putting down Indians who chose to rebel. It is for this reason that I suppose the most moving of all the memorials out there are the regimental badges in the Khyber Pass. They appear at intervals beside bends on that mountainous road, and they are generally grouped companionably in clumps. In one of these the Dorset Regiment, the Royal Sussex Regiment, the Essex Regiment, the South Wales Borderers, the Cheshire Regiment and the Gordon Highlanders stand together just above the track. The Tommies cast these replicas of their badges in concrete, then painted them so that the designs should stand out; and when I saw them in 1983, the last coat of paint couldn't have been more than twelve months old. What was it about those damned imperialists that inspired such generosity in the sons of men who had never ceased to battle the British along the Khyber, right up to the end in 1947? Plain guts? Fighting qualities? Something admirable besides?

Soldiers and civilians frequently left their bones on the sub-continent, and graveyards from the frontier down to Cape Comorin perpetuate the memory of our Raj. The inscriptions on these tombs are generally lugubrious, sometimes resounding, and rarely anything else. An exception, and the one I cherish most, is the grave I failed to find after a blistering morning's search in the thick undergrowth of the Christian cemetery in Peshawar. According to my guide book, its inscription says:

'Here lies Captain Ernest Bloomfield. Accidentally shot by his Orderly, March 2nd, 1879. "Well done, good and faithful servant."'

Some of the marks the British laid on this sub-continent were nothing to laugh at, but their worst characteristics departed with them 40 years ago. What they left behind has touched the life of just about every Indian and Pakistani, permanently, it seems. If at no other point, that claim could be sustained by noting that it was Dr Campbell of the Indian Medical Service who introduced the sub-continent to tea in 1941, since when it has become the national drink of rich and poor alike. But the most important legacy by far was the English language, which has enabled even the mildly educated to communicate across India as nothing else can (in a land with 15 major tongues, regional secession has more than once been threatened at the prospect of New Delhi imposing Hindi nationwide).

Though it's all very well to invoke military sentimentality of the frontier as evidence that the sub-continentals live easily with the reach-me-down of our imperialism, it's harder to gauge the reaction of the populace at large, especially now, as fewer and fewer natives have a memory of the Raj, and a visiting Englishman must seem not much different from a touring German to the majority of folk in the street. Those statues on the Calcutta maidan were, in fact, removed not long after I saw them there, and placed in less prominent surroundings out at suburban Barrackpore. A communist administration had been elected to form the state government of West Bengal, and the imperial bronzes were instantly put in their place.

But, hush, for I have quite recently seen a sight to gladden any old imperialist's eye. In that same torrid city stands the Great Eastern Hotel, which Kipling used to frequent when he came down from Lahore. Years ago it passed from private hands into those of the state government; which means that nowadays it is run by dutiful Bengali communists. In the lobby is a textile gift shop, on whose window is written in a curve of gilt letters cast in low relief – 'By permission of HM the King Emperor and HM the Queen Empress', all gleaming under a royal coat of arms. Which the government employees polish assiduously each day.

Now that's the response of Civilised Man!

CROSSING TO THE OTHER SIDE

The best way to see the Hebrides is from the deck of a boat. Only then can you take in the full beauty of these enchanted isles. The Victorians and Edwardians relished the sea. The wealthy had not the executive jets, but graceful yachts; glittering vessels of white and gold which moved like swans about the waters of the west.

For the not-so-wealthy in the age before the charabanc and the car you could voyage the length and breadth of the islands for shillings,

137

courtesy of David Macbrayne and his fleet of fast steamers. It was these
boats with their familiar black, red-banded funnels and names like
Loch Seaforth, *Hebrides*, *Fusilier*, *Chieftain* and *Clansman*, trailing
smoke and churning the sea, which linked all the islands together in a vital
network. Everything that was essential, from fencing wire and sheep dip
to oatmeal and sugar, came from the mainland by sea. At the beginning of
summer mothers brought their children back from lowland towns to get
colour in their cheeks on the family croft. The arrivals and departures
were as regular, almost, as clockwork. As the boat came round the
headland everyone made their way down to the stone pier to exchange
news and establish just who was coming ashore and what was their
business. In the spring the steamer took away the young cattle for
fattening on the mainland; in July it was the wool that went and in the
autumn the sheep. The boats punctuated the week and their comings and
goings were more important than the calendar itself.

I miss the boat very much. Today Macbrayne's has a highly utilitarian
fleet of car ferries which operate among the islands, but many communities
have long since lost their sea link and their piers lie rotting and unvisited.
In Portree, the tiny capital of the Isle of Skye, the whole life of the
village focused on the late afternoon arrival of the steamer which met
the Inverness train at Kyle of Lochalsh. The mail from the south was
on board and in summer the boat was packed with tourists and visitors.
And it was the same in small towns and villages throughout the west
– you didn't get your news from papers or the wireless but down on the
pier waiting for the boat.

The boats themselves were so solidly constructed that they outlived
whole generations. The *Claymore* was launched in 1881 and served the
islands summer and winter, battling up and down the Minch until she
was taken away, protesting no doubt, to be broken up in 1931. In
August 1925 my mother carried me, a six-week-old bundle, on board the
Glencoe which by then was in her 79th year of service. With the single

funnel, for'ard mast, great splashing paddles and bridge open to the elements she was as much a part of history as the Cuillins themselves. Like all the Macbrayne boats she was a tough old workhorse. She had first class accommodation, second and third – if you travelled third you were frequently not alone. A notice down there said: 'This cabin has accommodation for 90 passengers when not occupied by cattle, sheep, cargo or other encumbrances.'

It was not just the boats that were full of tradition and character but so were their daunting skippers. No captain of a Boeing wields the power and the authority of a Macbrayne man gold-braided on his bridge. Tales were told over the peat fire of their wit and the way they dealt with the condescending English. Most notorious of all was Captain 'Squeaky' Robertson. Two spinsters waylaid him on a gangway when the boat was passing the sea stacks known as Macleod's Maidens.

"Captain Robertson," said one of the ladies, "why are those rocks called Macleod's Maidens?"

"Well I wouldn't be knowing," replied Squeaky, "but one thing is certain, nobody's ever been up them!"

And then there was Captain Baxter of the Glencoe. On hearing the cry "Minister overboard!" he called down from the bridge "What denomination?" The answer was "Wee Free". Baxter leapt without a moment's hesitation to the engine-room telegraphs and rang them to Full Speed Ahead.

These men were the life-enhancing folk heroes of the Hebrides. It was they who got through to isolated communities in the wildest weather when lesser men would have run for safety and lesser boats would have sunk. Macbrayne was a lifeline of paramount importance; without those boats and the regularity of their arrival few communities could have survived. No wonder there was a love-hate relationship between islanders and their link with the rest of the world, a dependence which burst out in the memorable quatrain:

'The earth belongs unto the Lord
And all that it contains
Except the Western Highlands
And they are all Macbrayne's.'

But Macbrayne's certainly did its stuff. In Edwardian times there were tempting itineraries and round trips which could be as brief as two days or as long as a week. There was a week's cruise from Glasgow to Stornoway and back for £4 including all meals. The food was all freshly cooked on board. Porridge, kippers and bacon and egg when you rose; fresh fish for lunch, perhaps, or roast beef with mutton broth to warm you up, and another big meal at six. Travelling round the islands you became a part of the Gaelic way of life. As you moved from pier to pier your progress may have been leisurely but you felt the rain and the wind on your cheek and you smelt the sea. Even lonely St Kilda had a scheduled summer service; now the only way to get there is by joining one of the National Trust work parties.

When visitors leave Skye now it's by car. But when I was a child you got up early in the morning and if it was late in the year you would make your way down to the pier just as the light was breaking. Waving goodbye to relatives and friends was a misery. Summer was gone and you had a lifetime to wait before the steamer brought you back again:

'The daylight strengthens and the sirens sound;
The last rope splashes and the engines churn;
The quayside fades. O misty isle, it seems
As if no time to leave thee could be found
More fitting than the hour in which men turn
From sleeping, and, reluctant, lose their dreams.'
(Rev J. F. Marshall)

6

Passing Sentences

REST IN PEACE

T he world has never been quite the same since they stopped
advertising garden sheds on the back of *Radio Times*.

Every week without fail, the good shedmakers of Batley
would lay out their wares for the perusal of the nation in one of those
wonderfully fussy and action-packed displays where the layout artist
appeared to be trying to cut up an entire Dostoevsky novel and paste
it, with pictures, into the confines of an A3 page.

It was the prime advertising spot in the land. We all looked at *Radio Times*, and we all looked at it every day. And the great thing about the Batley ad was it was so densely informative on the matter of sheds that its study could easily while away the half-hour of 'Radio Newsreel' until 'Dick Barton – Special Agent' came on.

And why, you are entitled to wonder, did the manufacturers of the stout cedar Suffolk (with optional window) and the bombproof concrete Rutland (erected in under a day) feel it was worth shelling out, week after week, for the most expensive solus display spot in the entire media to shift stocks of something so prosaically mundane as a garden shed?

The answer is a great and universal truth that Einstein would have been happy to stumble upon had he put his mind to it instead of slaving away over all those sums just to arrive at such a tiny little equation: garden sheds have to do with a great deal more than gardening. In fact, they don't really have much to do with gardening at all. What they have to do with is the raising to the status of a religion the fine art of doing nothing.

The garden shed was the common man's Temple of Idleness, in which he could cast out the devils of Enthusiasm and worship instead at the feet of the gods Whittle, Footle, Doodle and Fiddle. Cocooned in a womb of serenity, far from prying eyes that would have him mend dripping taps or bend his mind to booking next year's holiday, a man could achieve a state of transcendental inactivity with the aid of nothing more complex than a cracked flowerpot in need of repair and a tranny tuned to the cricket.

Many a garden shed bought from the back of *Radio Times* was destined for an allotment. And what were allotments for? Growing organic vegetables? Not a bit of it; they were for watching organic vegetables grow. Preferably from a pensioned-off armchair, bleeding horsehair from a multiplicity of wounds, in the doorway of your Suffolk (carriage free in mainland Britain). And you would never have described a potato as   143 organic anyhow; organic was any illness that three fingers of Sanatogen tonic wine couldn't cure.

Allotments used to be sanctuaries where the truly idle could meet like minds and wallow in the comforting certainty of group inactivity. They were like naturist beaches; you don't feel a fool in your nothings if every other Jack and Jill around you has cast off the clouts – provided that the Great Dressed Majority are kept at least binocular distance away. Oh yes, and allotments had their Peeping Toms too; as urchins we used to snigger through gaps in the hawthorn hedge at old men in flat caps making pipe smoke like the Bismarck on the run while their cabbages almost creaked with rampant growth.

Alas, the world has been overtaken by earnestness. Now it is Volvo drivers who queue up at their local council office to inherit an allotment, not in search of a piece of hallowed ground for the pursuit of catatonic idleness, but to keep one step ahead of Sainsbury in their quest for the Utterly Untainted Aubergine. Former havens of peace are being desecrated by Enthusiasm, by people who have got into their head the distorted notion that doing nothing is a waste of life.

It can be no accident that, in this earnest era, garden sheds no longer appear on the back page of our biggest-selling weekly journal. The modern-day equivalent would be for the shed-makers of Batley to buy electronic prime time, like the entire two-minute break in 'News At Ten'. But no; shed advertising has gone, if not quite underground, then certainly off the back pages and into, well, more specialist publications.

If the Monstrous Regiment of the Earnest continue to have their way, it will be a case of leaning across the counter to the newsagent in conspiratorial fashion and asking *sotto voce* from the side of the mouth: "Er, you haven't got *Sheds Monthly*, have you?" To which, if he is a kindred spirit in idleness, he will whisper back: "Right here under the counter, squire. And if you're interested, I've a catalogue of do-it-yourself Danish garden buildings just in this morning. Strong stuff; don't let the wife see it."

Sheds have a great many virtues, of which two come to mind. First you cannot jog or indulge in any other form of supremely silly and damaging gymnastics in a shed; any properly run-in shed will be far too full of clutter to take more than one and a half steps without poking yourself in the eye with a six-foot length of lavatory overflow pipe which might just come in handy one day.

Secondly, there are now so many earnestly serious Sunday newspapers of such size that, unless you purchased the huge all-cedar Wensleydale (stores garden tools, mowers and has room for a workshop), there is no possibility of getting them all into a shed at once to read. These very newspapers are against the spirit of an idler age, with their po-faced view of a world in which everything seems to matter, and yet they are a curious paradox; by the time you have read their endless leisure supplements stuffed with ideas of what to do with your free time, there is no time left to do it. They are, in their way, groping towards an ideal of idleness.

We writers appreciate garden sheds, yet our craft teaches us to snatch periods of advanced pointlessness, like Winston snatching forty winks while running the Battle of Britain, in any situation. All that is needed is a blank sheet of paper and an urgent job to do. Faced with a deadline and not a single idea, writers can become world-class footlers. Cleaning the typewriter keys is much favoured; my own speciality, in the days of manual writing machines, was to polish the chrome-plated carriage return lever on my portable.

And always, in the end, after a really good footle or doodle, the idea would come. I never yet met a man who was pole-axed by a good idea while dressed in a bright green tracksuit pounding the guts out of his knee and hip joints on a city pavement. If James Watt had had a kettle in his garden shed, that's where he would have invented the steam engine.

When you see the very old interviewed on television on the occasion of their 105th birthday, does a single one of them ever look like the type who had spent so much as a day of their lives jogging or reading the *Independent on Sunday*? Not a bit of it; they all look to me like people who had sheds.

Now look here, I've got better things to do this Sunday morning than sit here lecturing you on the moral and physical benefits of wasting time. I've got a trowel to polish, and I think it's in the shed.

ENGLISH TO THE END

"You are American?" the French barber whom I was trying to prevent cropping me like a visiting Fulbright professor said to me at the time of the Profumo affair. "No, English." "Ah well," he looked at me with pity, "there are good and bad in every country."

In the age of the Englishman such a conversation would have been unthinkable. The "No, English" would have emerged like a trumpet blast, instead of the faint note of apology which was all that I could manage. It would have been thundered forth in our native tongue, instead of being muttered in French in what was clearly taken for a Boston accent by a man in a Swedish shirt, Spanish leather coat and trousers from Cecil Gee. And it would have sent the same barber in the Rue St Honoré scurrying for the clippers instead of feeling for a tone of patronising sympathy.

When Mr Profumo lied his way out of the limelight, when Mr Macmillan waved a pale hand and muttered "La commedia e finito" in the tones of Bulldog Drummond about to face Carl Peterson for the last time, the Englishman became extinct. I feel enough sympathy for him to now place a few plastic poppies and a flat whisky and soda on his grave, confident that we shall not see his like again.

Lord Byron, Sherlock Holmes, Nelson, Wellington, Jeeves, Macmillan, Bertie Wooster, Palmerston, Dr Crippen, Hamlet, Mrs Pankhurst, D. H. Lawrence, Lady Hester Stanhope, Melbourne, Shelley and Neville George Clevely Heath – the list can be prolonged, but the qualities remain the same. There is something fictional about the Englishman. Even when he really existed he did so in a realm of fantasy. This was his strength. Wrapped in the curious mists of his own eccentricity, the dangers of the outside world – the hangman, Claudius the King, the charging Zulus, the forcible feeders, or the political threat of models on the make – had only the effect on him of dreams. And he himself was a character of such manifest absurdity, so outrageously confident in his illusion of security, that the world drew back before him, often helpless with laughter – which only turned to rage and indignation when it was discovered that he had got his own way again.

If it should be objected that this is a class-conscious definition of the departed Englishman, this is true. Class, mystic, tribal, illogical and mad, was his great obsession; the more so when he came from what he rather uncharmingly called the working classes. Not that class was anything to be enjoyed, revelled in or boasted about; it was usually a source of extreme discomfort, like the piercing draughts which howled under the doors of the best houses. In the classless, international world everyone has central heating.

My own slight feeling of waste may come from the fact that I was trained as an Englishman and then let out into a world where he no longer existed. "Don't put butter on your hair," the headmaster of my preparatory school solemnly warned us in a period when history was being made in Munich, Czechoslovakia and Spain. "Ghurka regiments frequently butter their hair. The stuff goes rancid and causes an unpleasant odour on a hot parade ground." He was a tall, beautiful old man with long white, wavy hair and the mad blue eye of the prophet Isaiah. He would summon us to meals by playing hymn tunes on a small carillon of bells, an occupation which so fascinated him that he would carry on playing until long after our brief and disgusting meal was over, and we were kept from sleep by the distant tinkle of 'Onward Christian Soldiers'. On Armistice Day he preached us a sermon, out on a windy field by the river, in which he talked of Passchendaele as if it were some ancient First Eleven match. Bored with this we used to lean back on our heels, let our minds go a complete blank and force ourselves to faint.

Learning to faint on Armistice Day seems, looking back on it now, the most practical lesson of our vanished English education. In order to preserve the Englishman's feeling of calm superiority in the face of the universe, it was essential that he shouldn't know too much about it; just as too much deep thought on the mathematical problems involved in riding a bicycle may lead you to fall off. When I look back on almost ten years spent with the grammar of defunct languages which I was never able to master, when I remember the weary jibes of my classics teacher at the smells and bangs which arose from the science department where those few pupils, too backward for the Greek subjunctive, were crouched over the Bunsen burner, I realise what I was being equipped for. Picking up some foreign bomb and throwing it back without any suspicion that it might go off.

Confidence was the key in politics which allowed the English to take such unpardonable liberties with the world; in our literature which was a riot of unblushing personal fantasies; and in our crimes which made the classic English murders hopeful, often romantic gestures of lonely self-assertion, the weird envy of every other nation. The history of the 1914 war is full of stories of helmeted English ladies, with their long overcoats and billy-cans of tea, tramping the shell-shocked moon landscape in order to tell some temporarily errant husband he must pull himself together and stop being missing, believed killed. To them death seemed foreign, and not quite to be taken seriously.

Of course, and quite rightly, it's all over now. It is comical to think of a few vanishing public schools still training the sons of self-sacrificing admen and superstore owners for life on a non-existent north-west frontier; but such training doesn't take as long as once it did. We went into Europe not like Byron, with dogs and monkey and a private doctor and a creaking carriage, to erect another untidy and eccentric Newstead Abbey, full of boxers and breakfast, on the Adriatic; but in our French shirts and Belgian blazers and rimless Swedish glasses. We now eat the same food on Cephalonia as we cook, off the colour supplement recipes, in Lancaster Gate. We now all, old and weary as we may grow, do our best to imitate the international swinging teenager who is finally as boring and indistinguishable as the international Hilton Hotel. And we now meekly concede, as the vanished Englishman never would, that there are good and bad in every country.

THE REST IS SILENCE

I once tuned in to 'Any Questions' and heard Lord Chalfont saying: "I can't say I'm attracted to pibroch music." I know the feeling. I spent five years at school in Scotland surrounded by people trying to play the bagpipes. I even spent a term trying to learn myself, out of curiosity, and found out that you can't even play all the notes of scale on the pipe. No wonder they all go red in the face.

"The sound they produce is outlandish and, to my ears, unmusical,"

151

continued the censorious Lord. "And to be quite honest, I can't really see
the point of the way they dress up in their slightly ridiculous uniforms,
except as a way of drawing attention to themselves." Actually the kilt, which
I had to wear from time to time, is not half a bad garment, nice and free
and easy; good to dance in, too, as I was later to find out. I just think that
Scotland is the wrong country for it, as it is so obviously a hot climate piece
of dress. But as far as the rest of the clobber was concerned, all the sashes,
feathers and things that people get up in to play the pipes, yes, I agreed with
him there.

"And I think it's just plain daft," concluded Chalfont, "the way they
dye their spiky hair blonde and put safety pins through their noses." This
left me in mid-air without an aeroplane. What was he talking about? What
kind of rebel pibroch bands had he been listening to? Or had he finally
gone round the twist? "No," he summed up, "I don't like punk rock
music."

Blimey, I had misheard punk rock as pibroch. There couldn't be two
kinds of music more different, and yet I had accepted what he said about
one as applying equally well to the other. What kind of intellectual was I?

Well, the normal kind of intellectual actually, because I immediately set
about sorting out the facts to fit in with my ideas and came to the
conclusion that pibroch is just as objectionable as punk rock when we
normally hear it: that is, when we don't want to. Music is pumped at us in all
sorts of circumstances when it is not natural to hear music – in lifts, railway
stations, pubs, hotel lobbies, aeroplanes – and the effect on me is to turn me
from an inoffensive, early middle-aged wishy-washy liberal into an
apoplectic old colonel. I know, I know, this is not a new complaint.

I once wrote to the Stationmaster of Waterloo – Area Manager, he's
called now – to object violently to the loud music relayed through his
otherwise quite pleasant terminus, echoing round the roof like some bad
1930s sound-track. He wrote back, noting my determination to travel only

northward by trains until he reversed his policy on Southern Region, and stating his belief that most people seemed to like it.

He's quite wrong. Most people don't notice it, any more than they notice the colour of wallpaint or the smell of car fumes. Most people don't notice it, because they don't even like music particularly. Thomas Beecham said: "The British don't like music, but they love the noise it makes." In similar vein, Robert Morley remembers how as a child he was wheeled by his nanny along the sea-front at Folkestone, down a stretch where you could hear simultaneously two brass bands on the promenade playing quite different compositions. "Don't talk to me about discos," he concluded, "I have heard the real thing."

The only explanation for the bombardment of pre-recorded music is that it has become another soft drug; people reach out for it in the same way that they reach for another filter cigarette, that is, without thinking. It is an audible sleeping tablet, or perhaps a light stimulant. What they don't do is listen to it. The only people who listen to it are people who are interested in music and they are the very ones who dislike it, because they notice the vacuousness of it.

The odd thing is that things sounded perfectly nice before canned music came along. The rattle of conversation and laughter, chinking and drinking, in an English pub forms a very pleasant background noise. The sounds made in a restaurant by knives and forks, by bottles pouring, by waiters dropping twenty plates just inside the kitchen and the rest of the staff laughing at him, are perfectly adequate without the addition of Somebody's Silver Strings. And I actively like the noise of a railway station: the going and coming of trains, the banging of doors, the crashing of trolleys, the quiet calm of a porter leaning on a trolley marked For Passenger Use Only, the ricocheting of all these sounds round the roof. Why smother it in canned music? For the same reason that the British like smothering their food in bottled sauce?

I remember once hearing a play on BBC radio set in a family whose

153

mother was deaf and yet who was a tremendously placid and contented soul. Then one day she found a course of treatment which cured her deafness. For the first time she realised what a contentious and embittered lot her family were – arguments, complaints and back-stabbing all day long. Her placidity vanished the more she had to listen to it all, until one day she voluntarily gave up her treatment and relapsed into a contented deafness.

I know how she feels. I had a slight ear infection last week which left my hearing very muffled. At last I could walk down Oxford Street without hearing the flashy denim funk coming out of every jeans shop. I could go to my hairdresser without being too conscious of Capital Radio and travel by train without hearing the drip drip drip of the drums coming out of the badly-named personal stereo systems. I even thought of paying a sentimental, unhearing trip to Waterloo Station for old times' sake.

It's cleared up now. Pity. Another few months and I could have avoided the tinny recording of Christmas carols blasting out in Kensington High Street. Meanwhile, I am reminded of the words of a scientist who recently analysed the contents of the River Rhine and found it tremendously polluted. "So the water of the Rhine is now unsafe?" the interviewer asked him. The expert hesitated. "Actually, there are so many chemicals in the river that scientifically speaking you can't really describe its contents as water at all." Artistically speaking, I don't think you can describe the contents of most loudspeakers as music at all. I just wish it didn't have to drip into my ears and cause brain infection.

· ·

MUSIC'S DEATHLY HUSH

I am not musical. I learned that the hard way. Ssh! That was my father listening to Brahms, Chopin or Stravinsky, Caruso perhaps, I don't remember. As a kid everybody went 'Ssh' when listening to classical music. You don't speak, you don't even whisper, or play with your bricks or your miniature railway, you just sit still in utter silence. Classical music was near to God. My father sometimes played the flute.

Now my mother was hooked on the piano, had studied under a

well-known organist and in this feminist age might have turned
professional. She had high hopes for her son, so we got to work on the
piano-scales and tears.

That was how music and I fell out. A pact – no more piano, no more
tears. But I was a sad disappointment to her, and if you have ever been
a sad disappointment at the age of five or six, you will understand. I now
disliked music. I had it again at my first boarding school and have a
mental photo-flash recollection of a dozen small boys gathered round the
piano and a large soprano-looking woman making us sing 'Where the
bee sucks there suck I', which even at that age seemed an odd form of
self-expression.

If I disliked it so much, then why in the world, you may ask, am I
writing about music, particularly if you happen to know a lot about
it, something that I certainly do not. But don't abandon me now. The
story of the convert is always worth hearing, particularly since my
conversion was all of a part with a complete revolution in the attitude
to music in this country.

Words being my forte, a bed-sit in Bloomsbury found me musically
equipped with a liking for Noel Coward and Gertie Lawrence, a range
that extended from 'Nymph Errant' to an upper limit of Gilbert and
Sullivan. And later, nobody having apparently thought fit to produce
any good marching songs in the Twenties and Thirties, it was on
'Tipperary', 'Pack up your Troubles', 'Mademoiselle from
Armentières', not to mention 'Dead-eyed Dick' and the 'Ball of
Kirriemuir', that I went to war in World War II, expanding my lungs
– tonelessly of course. But in a mêlée of men, all singing like crazy, and
the thump of feet, you can let yourself go, however uneven your
singing.

Then the desert and Josephine Baker. I will always remember that
extraordinary evening, out in the open right by our tents. She was such
a personality – singing, cracking jokes with a thousand sweaty sodgers

in an earthy mixture of French and English, and the flat of the Western Desert all about her for miles and bloody miles.

Josephine, and others who came out to entertain us, loosened the strings of music, but it was Italy that really changed us all, the mean streets of Napoli, where every woman had a marvellous voice, no gardez-loo or even a break in the singing as the slops came down. And it wasn't just O Sole Mio they sang, it was bits and pieces of Verdi, Rossini, Puccini et al, and when those with money and the right contacts went to the opera, it was not to sit in silent awe, but to meet their friends, gossip and have an evening out – *silenzio* only for the tenor or the prima donna they had come to hear give their renderings of particular arias.

On one occasion we entertained the reigning prima donna in our mess. She was so large that when she was sprawled on the stage and had to be lifted, it usually required two male singers to get her on her feet again. She arrived with three or four beautiful Neapolitan girls in tow, plus her manager, and having demolished a fortnight's ration of 'bully', she was persuaded to sing. I doubt whether her voice was properly trained (most of the real stars had gone north with the Germans), but she had the most powerful voice of any woman I have ever heard, and though the rooms were big, we were most of us driven to listen to her from the corridor outside! But nobody said Ssh and it was all great fun.

Music was suddenly for enjoyment, the hushed awe of childhood gone for ever.

In Rome we had Aïda staged in the massive ruins of the Basilica close by the Roman Forum, and in the theatre proper we had marvellously variegated programmes, say the first act of *Traviata*, five smash hits any one of which Rodgers, Berlin or Gershwin would have been happy to have dreamed up for a musical; then a concert for the next act, the prelude to an opera say, followed by *Bolero*, something popular, then part of a symphony, Beethoven perhaps, in short, a musical pot pourri that had us all enthralled by its variety; and for the final act, 30 minutes or so of ballet, *Swan Lake*, *Petrushka*, anything they had costumes for and dancers. We all loved it. I met Gigli and had a long talk with him and his daughter, and came away from the overheated flat with the realisation that the voice requires a lot of cosseting, that singing, like writing, requires a lot of practice.

It was Italy more than any other theatre of war that opened a whole new world to something close on a million of our men and women, and it was after their return home that music as a popular entertainment really took off, so that now Britain is one of the world's great centres of music, and even I have my radio almost permanently tuned to Radio 3.

But with classical music on radio an irritating habit has developed – biographical diarrhoea. Each composition is now almost always prefaced by its history or the composer's life story, even his idiosyncrasies given in such detail that sometimes you feel you know what he had for breakfast the morning he first appeared in Vienna, Berlin, Paris, London or New York. It's irritating because all I want is to listen to the music. Doubly irritating because readers of my books are not informed of my breakfast fads, and on the media, if a writer hasn't got it in his contract, the poor devil may not even get a mention as they reproduce the words he has sweated so hard to string together. And if his work is set to music, then like as not the singer will so distort the vowels that the words become unintelligible.

Sour grapes? Of course. But Gilbert had to fight very hard to train a company to enunciate his words sufficiently to put the humour of his lines across. Not so, of course, Sullivan his music. As for the biographical outpourings composed by the courtiers of classical music, I just wish to say to them – *Ssh*!

THE COMING OF AGE

This year I turned 60, which somehow seems enormously older than a sprightly 59. At one leap, or, more honestly, with an arthritic shuffle, I have passed from the dignity of middle age to the pathos of old age. Grateful as we poor old folk must be to receive financial rewards for our longevity, it is painful to bear the stigma of being 'senior', divided for ever from those of our fellows who rank themselves under an opposing or junior banner.

Still worse is it to become officially known as a 'citizen', potential fodder for a future Simon Schama. Webster's Dictionary confirms my suspicion that the original sense of this frenchified word is one who lived in a city, a distasteful sobriquet for an inveterate country-dweller like myself. (Can the word be used here in a prospective sense, announcing in advance the day when we are carted off to old age homes in the city?) Citizen also means, says Webster, a member of a state, one owing allegiance to a government and entitled to protection from it. That 'from' is nicely ambiguous. And finally, it can mean a civilian, 'as opposed to a soldier or a policeman', still further humiliation in being now formally debarred from membership in these noble professions. I am suffused with wrath and self-pity!

But what am I lamenting? Certainly not youth itself. Who would wish to return to that condition of uneasy potential, when one was continually being put to the test? Even if one was 'good at exams', and romped through them with a horrid exhilaration, this constant exposure to judgment was of its very nature disconcerting. Every year not only revealed to others how one was to be classified, but it seduced an internal acceptance of the classification as objectively valid, and hence, all too often, self-fulfilling.

The verdicts of our youth are dangerous: blessed maturity which provides so many elegant and acceptable disguises. Nor would one want again the uncertainties of youth, when goals had to be chosen and sometimes binding choices made, all ignorantly. At 60 we have at least arrived, perhaps not where we meant to go, but at least somewhere. And having arrived we can build and cultivate, released from the fret of travel. (Travelling hopefully is better than arrival only if we are moving in the wrong direction.) We are only becoming in youth, in both senses of the word. The solidity of being, and being in secret, that blessed non-testable state of post academia, may lack charm but is infinitely restful.

160　　　No, what I regret is not youth itself but the freedom we had then to make a decision and take it for granted that the body would implement our choice. Money may have been a problem then, and perhaps time, but given the necessities, all depended upon our sole decision. A day at the Tate? No problem. An all-night vigil or an all-night party, a pilgrimage round the Romanesque churches of France and Spain, a hike in the Lake District, hour upon hour of play rehearsals: given the opening, we simply put our psychic horse at the jump and the physical meekly complied. In fact, there seemed to be only one horse, one single thundering steed which obeyed our commands; tiredness, mental exhaustion, these were states we acknowledged with little sympathy and soon shrugged off. 'To be or not to be'; it can only be the question for a young Hamlet (40 of course being young to the old age of 60). These broad clear decisions become progressively difficult as the body ceases its obedience. That ill-directed freedom is what we so mournfully recognise as lost for ever as we grow old. But it is hard to remember that our will is no longer dominant, more especially since one of the other characteristics of our advanced years is that the will has firmed and toughened with practice. What we want now we want with an incomparable force. We can bring to bear on our desires an experienced intelligence, that knows precisely what we want and why we want it, that is skilled in the intricacies of manoeuvring or even (though I confess this with shame) of manipulating. One has learned, painfully but well, which strings need pulling and which need shearing.

All the apparatus for implementing our will is beautifully in place. And what do we find? That the wretched body falters, our ancient energies flag. We have struggled up the arduous slopes within reach of the astral goal, and our muscles refuse service. We can no longer rely upon the body, and the mind too begins to invalidate itself. We may not be senile, we heroes of the senior citizenship, but we may sometimes find a haze where once there was sharp clarity.

Of course, some citizens are more senior than others: the fortunate may well be in their prime as they move deeper into their sixties. I speak of myself, tottering on, well enough but basically enfeebled.

Maybe it is as well. Such is the as yet unrealised potential for self-determination within us all, that it may be a mercy for mankind that the will to power becomes unrealisable. Our personal interiorised Napoleon is probably better off in the Elba of our incapacities. Let the juniors be grateful for their deliverance.

PICTURE ACKNOWLEDGMENTS

Hulton Picture Company: *3, 11, 15, 19, 24, 34, 43, 47, 51, 56, 60, 70, 78, 82, 88, 92, 96, 101, 105, 114, 118, 122, 142, 147, 151, 155, 159.*

Popperfoto: *127, 132.*

The Bettmann Archive: *65.*

John Vickers: *7.*

Victoria and Albert Museum: *74.*

The Still Moving Picture Co: *137.*

Press Association: *39.*

Peter Whyte: *109.*